Meeting Triumph
and Disaster

Meeting Triumph and Disaster

How Milton Shedd helped to win World War II, found Sea World, conserve his beloved ocean, and pass on the values that fueled his success.

"If you can meet with Triumph and Disaster and treat those two impostors just the same… yours is the Earth and everything that's in it, and—which is more—you'll be a Man, my son!" —Rudyard Kipling

CONOR FRIEDERSDORF

ISBN 069278554X
ISBN 13: 9780692785546
Library of Congress Control Number: 2016916475
California, Costa Mesa, CA

Dedication

This book is dedicated to the memory of Milton C. Shedd, to his wife, Peggie, and to the men and women of the World War II generation, who made the world we inhabit possible before entrusting us with it.

About the Author

Conor Friedersdorf is a staff writer at *The Atlantic*, a contributor to the *Los Angeles Times*, and founding editor of The Best of Journalism, a newsletter dedicated to exceptional nonfiction.

Author's
Acknowledgements

Particular thanks go to Milt's children, Steve, Carol, and Bill, who provided unfettered access to the private papers, letters, photographs, and family history of their father; to Milt's grandchildren, who were generous in the personal stories they shared of their family's patriarch; to my wife, Courtney, for her edits and patience as I completed this project; and to James Carmichael, Lee Friedersdorf, and James Poulos, whose edits at various stages were indispensable.

Foreword

The exploits of Milt Shedd first piqued my interest at 13, when a P.E. teacher asked everyone in my freshman class to take turns introducing ourselves. A kid whose name I have since forgotten told a long story about catching a big fish. Milt's grandson was up next. "Hi, I'm Cody," he said. "My grandpa caught Shamu." Everyone took it as a joke and laughed.

We never suspected that the truth was even more incredible–that while Cody's grandfather did not literally catch Shamu, he did found Sea World; catch many of the marine creatures that filled its original tanks; and led the company from its birth to its emergence as a world famous attraction.

As my friendship with Cody deepened, I gradually learned that his grandfather's life story was filled with amazing exploits: helping his family to survive the Great Depression; literal death-defying heroics behind Japanese lines in World War II; pioneering conservation efforts that aided the survival of several West Coast fishes. Every so often, during the hours we spent hanging out in high school, Cody would reveal yet another fascinating fact. And as much as any particular story, I was always struck by the way that my normally irreverent friend spoke of his grandfather: with a mix of awe, pride, and respect that couldn't help but make a powerful impression, because the more I learned about the values and life lessons that Cody's grandfather handed down, the more I was struck by how similar they were to the values of my own grandparents.

Years later, when the Shedd family hired me to write Milt's biography, the project appealed to me not only because of Milt's worldly accomplishments and my fascination with the time period in California in which he lived, but because his values were, in many respects, representative of a generation that shaped our world and our respective families. As that generation passes from the scene, I liked the idea of setting down not just their notable exploits, but the attitudes and values that shaped them. There was no one in The Greatest Generation more explicit about those values, or more determined to pass them on, than Milt Shedd. And because he so valued independent thinking and frank appraisals, his progeny were the rare sorts who did not want hagiography—they saw value in preserving his life story just as he lived it.

With their help, I captured Milt as accurately and completely as I could, confident that his strengths and weaknesses alike can help all who read his story to glean wisdom from it.

Conor Friedersdorf
Venice, California
Summer 2016

Table of Contents

One

CHAIRMAN MILT

Hours before posing for the most daring photograph of his life, Milton C. Shedd donned a suit, knotted a conservative necktie, and drove from his Newport Beach home to Sea World, the San Diego oceanarium that he cofounded. His tenure as its longtime Chairman of the Board carried an unusual perk: access to marine creatures that had fascinated and delighted him since childhood. Executives at other companies sat for publicity stills beside corporate logos. Milt would stand beside the pool where Shamu and her successors performed. At first, all went according to plan. A 5-ton orca glided to the water's edge, popped her torso into the air, and let her tongue peek out. Milt leaned down as if to get a kiss.

Handsome even in his sixties, he smiled alongside Sea World's most iconic performer. Then he dove into the water beside her.

The plunge was decades in the making. Most Americans never see an orca outside of captivity. But Milt, a lifelong fisherman, first encountered them in the wild, where he marveled at their social intelligence, playfulness, and ruthlessness. Shamu's arrival only increased his fascination. He took every opportunity to question Sea World veterinarians about what knowledge they were gleaning from one of the earliest captive killer whales. Posing in Shamu Stadium that day, he knew the water's salt content, its depth, and how different its tamed inhabitants were from their wild cousins. Sea World orcas performed multiple times daily for thousands of spectators in San Diego, Orlando, and Ohio, largely without incident. Back then, during the 1980s, the park had yet to experience a fatality. Serious injuries were rare.

Of course, Sea World orcas remained wild creatures. And Milt understood that even the most carefully taught animals could hurt their minders. This inherent risk was outweighed in his mind by the faith that he had in Sea World's training staff, his sense of their overall safety record, and his desire to get wet. He stripped off his business attire and donned a trainer's wetsuit. Submerged moments later, he showed no sign of anxiety, even hanging onto the 5-ton whale as it circled the pool. For most men, the tow would have been thrill enough. But as it ended, Milt made one last request. Could the photographer get a shot of the killer whale soaring over his head?

Born in El Paso, Texas, on September 26, 1922, Milton Cicero Shedd lived zealously for 79 years and died with few regrets. For decades, he told everyone he knew that marrying his wife, Peggie, was the smartest thing he ever did. He delighted most in their three children, their ten grandchildren, and his greatest passion: sportfishing. His family reckons that he spent 3,500 days, or almost 10 years, on the ocean. His skill was unsurpassed.

Publicly, he is best known for the marine park that he created with three partners. During two decades as Chairman of the Board, he raised the bulk of the capital needed to build Sea World San Diego; oversaw every aspect of the enterprise; shepherded the young company through major recessions; presided over its expansions into Florida and Ohio; and helped to avert a hostile takeover. When his tenure ended in 1985, Sea World was the most famous oceanarium in the world. Visited by tens of millions, it had forever changed humanity's relationship to the ocean and marine mammals, inspiring new affection for orcas, new efforts to conserve their habitat, and ultimately, protests against keeping them in captivity.

For Milt, Sea World meant financial security, a *New York Times* obituary, and a nickname, The Walt Disney of the Sea, likening him to an icon. Yet the oceanarium is far from his only legacy. In World War II, his success in combat helped him to become one of the youngest army captains in the Pacific theater. While serving as an infantry officer in the Solomon Islands, he volunteered to lead an intelligence patrol far behind Japanese lines. Sneaking single-file through dense jungle his dozen men found a camp where the enemy outnumbered them almost two-to-one. "As a result of Lieutenant Shedd's gallant, well-planned action," says the Silver Star citation issued by President Roosevelt, "twenty-three of the enemy, the entire group, were killed without loss of any of our troops."

Milt's obituary in the *Los Angeles Times* emphasized the non-profit research foundation that he created, calling it his "lasting legacy to marine science and education." At first, his partners in Sea World were against funding what became the Hubbs-SeaWorld Research Institute. Their startup was cash-strapped, its success uncertain, and marine research struck them as extraneous. Milt insisted that it was both proper and savvy for a corporation to give back. A decade later, the research institute would help Sea World to persuade regulators that it served the public interest. Later, Milt's early emphasis on marine conservation was seen as prescient due to the global depletion of fish stocks and the non-profit's role in addressing the problem. Even in retirement, Milt raised significant sums for Hubbs and made a major bequest to UCLA, ensuring that both would work on behalf of the ocean long after his death.

Fishing stories may seem unimportant in comparison, but West Coast sportfishermen remember Milt in their telling. They marvel that he could spot the twin fins of a swordfish from three miles away if the ocean was flat and calm; that he once caught a marlin and a swordfish on the same day, a feat few anglers have equaled; and that his aim throwing a harpoon from a swordfish boat was deadly. Before he died, The International Game Fish Association inducted him into their angling hall of fame, where his portrait still hangs among fellow inductees Zane Grey and Ernest Hemingway.

The fishing trip dearest to Milt was a weeks-long expedition that he led off Baja California, where a small team sought fishes to fill the earliest Sea World aquariums. The techniques that they invented enabled them to collect creatures never before displayed for the public. Later, after a marine biology expert had taken over fish collection, Milt would escape from behind his desk whenever possible to spend time among the park's ever-expanding menagerie. Insatiably curious, he would question the staff at length. "What does this fish eat?" "How were these walruses caught?" "Why is it so difficult to keep these sharks alive in captivity?" And most memorably: "Would you have that orca leap up over my head?"

Thus his moment treading water; submerged to the neck; urging the trainer to give a signal; calm as the killer whale slipped into the depths. Now the orca was a shadow in the water, 10,000 pounds of muscle and teeth irrevocably set in motion. The photographer steadied his camera. The orca thrust upward, propelled herself airborne, soared over Milt in a parabolic leap—and WHOOSH–broke the surface distant enough to avoid thwacking him with a tail fluke bigger than any man. The photograph captured the orca at the apex of her leap. As she soared overhead Milt flashed a smile tinged with mischievous joy. His life was a series of calculated risks taken after long reflection and preparation.

The big ones all paid off.

Two

Discovering the Sea

*"It all began with a walk on the Santa Monica Pier
and a gaze into the water below. Milt Shedd saw a
school of smelt. He was instantly mesmerized. The
four-year-old longed to learn everything about smelt.
What did they eat? What ate them? Where do they go?
From that day forth, Milt spent a lifetime examining
the underwater world so full of life and mysteries,
sating an irresistible curiosity. A simple walk on the
pier as a child drove Milt Shedd into becoming one of
the most revered pioneers in marine conservation."*

– DAVE STREGE, THE ORANGE COUNTY REGISTER

During the 1920s, Santa Monica offered all the delights of summer. Its municipal pier hosted events most every weekend: a performing clown, a beauty contest sponsored by the American Legion, even a stunt motorcyclist launching himself into the ocean. An amusement pier was steps away—so close, in fact, that children ran from one pier to the other without noticing the seam. At 4, Milt would have marveled at the carousel carrying kids on hand-carved animals. The Whirlwind Dipper rollercoaster would have seemed like mountain ridges. There was a Ferris wheel, a swing ride, and ice cream for sale. Yet years later, when Milt recounted his earliest memories of Santa Monica, he included none of its amusements. He told of gazing down into the water, seeing smelt, and hating to go home, where he daydreamed about fishermen at the wooden rail.

Milt's father and namesake never saw the ocean in his own youth. Born in El Paso, Texas, in 1887, Milton Senior excelled in high school and studied engineering at the Illinois Institute of Technology, where he joined the Phi Kappa Sigma fraternity and worked on the yearbook. In 1909, back in El Paso, he bought a small business that made fire escapes, window guards, and ornamental wrought iron. And he courted Ruth Winslow Critchett, the eldest in a family of daughters. The young couple wanted to wed in 1911, but delayed so that Milton Senior could pay off his business loan. During World War I, he worked as a construction supervisor at Fort Bliss and gathered intelligence in Mexico for the U.S. army.

Milton Senior and Ruth finally married after the war, honeymooning in the Chiricahua Mountains during the autumn of 1919. Ten months later, their eldest child, Ruthie, was born. They welcomed her into a middle class home, and less than two years later, when Ruth was pregnant again, a lucky accident blessed the family. "With a second child on the way, mother needed help," Ruthie recalled years later, "and the Mexican girl who normally helped her had not shown up for days."

A different young woman, Maria Meza, impressed the family during an interview to fill the vacant position, but was sent away at the last moment when the former helper unexpectedly returned. "What a shame," said Ruth's sister, who was present all the while. "That Maria would be so much better with the children." Realizing she was right, Ruth gave chase, catching Maria as she boarded a streetcar. Hired on the spot, Maria would live with the Shedds for six decades until her death.

That second child was named after his father. By the time little Milt was born, on September 26, 1922, Milton Senior was a trusted employee of the Robert E. McKee Construction Company, which would shape skylines across the southwest. Its principals saw that the oil, agriculture, and entertainment industries were combining to make Southern California an economic powerhouse, and asked Milton Senior to relocate so that he could oversee the company's first Golden State office. The Shedd family set off in a touring car sometime in early 1923, with Milton Senior at the wheel, Ruth beside him, and Ruthie in the backseat with Maria, who cradled baby Milt in her lap.

Today, traveling from El Paso to San Diego takes 110 minutes by air or twelve hours driving. Crossing the desert in the 1920s was an arduous journey. The dusty trip across New Mexico and Arizona took several days. Ahead lay the Old Plank Road, the original route connecting Yuma to San Diego. Motorists drove on one lane of wooden planks. There were many hazards: a dearth of water, small dunes that formed over the road, hard to predict flash floods. Traffic jams formed as cars negotiated awkward turnouts. One sardonic contemporary urged drivers to bring "extra boards, two auto jacks, gunny sacks, a shovel, food and water for at least two days, and—to be totally prepared—a set of boxing gloves."

The Shedds bounced toward their destination at 10 miles-per-hour, narrowly beating flash-floods that made theirs the last car to cross the route for days. They stayed in San Diego just long enough to add a final child, Irving, before Milton Senior's career brought them to settle permanently in Los Angeles. It is almost as if Milt was destined to grow up there at the edge of a continent: had he stayed in the desert, or spent his curious childhood gazing down a rugged mountainside or across a grass-covered prairie, his life would not have unfolded as it did, for the ocean touched most every part of it.

All the Shedds thrived in California. Even the children could see that Milton Senior and Ruth were smitten. An undated picture shows the young couple posing in front of the giant sequoias of the Mariposa Grove; the national park at Yosemite was a favorite vacation spot. The family's biggest problem was the travel demands of the construction industry: Milton Senior supervised projects all over the southwest.

"Don't let the kiddies forget their hardworking daddy—they are such precious youngsters," he began a letter postmarked San Bernardino. "I am anxious to make a lot of money the next few years so they will have what they need." He missed them dearly. "I am so happy when I am with you and the kiddies; it is not very pleasant to be away so many days," he wrote. "But you will all enjoy me so much more when I get home, and the money will come in mighty handy." He concluded, "I love you my darling girl, I love you," having urged the angels in heaven to "guard you and my precious little ones."

In 1927, the family bought a bungalow-style house at 1132 Stearns Drive near Pico and Fairfax. Ruth was thrilled to have a second bathroom. The kids delighted in the large backyard, a scene of many fond memories: there was Ruthie's playhouse, a wooden swing-set with metal rings for Milt to hang on, a surplus army tent that the neighborhood kids used to host improvised circus shows, and a small aviary that soon filled up with birds. Ruth kept house, joined the PTA as an officer, served on the local election board, and tended to the children, relying on Maria for domestic help and company.

Their neighborhood, Carthay Circle, was just five years old. The 136-acre tract had a church and a full-service grocery. The kids walked streets lined with sycamore, ash, and elm to the elementary school or to Carthay Circle Theater, a palace of Hollywood glamour ten minutes away on foot. The theater hosted premieres, once attracting a crowd of 30,000 people who hoped to see Snow White and the Seven Dwarfs. More typical were weekend features that did brisk but manageable business and matinee Westerns that Milt would attend on weekday afternoons. He sat up close to the screen; his older sister, friends in tow, would occupy a row farther back.

When in town, Milton Senior would drop his kids off at school, drive to work, and return home as late as 10 pm. Often he barely finished supper before dozing by the radio. The long hours prevented him from having a closer relationship with kids who adored him. Milt got in the habit of going to a neighbor's house and asking the man who lived there when he had a question about sports or animals.

His curiosity about the natural world was irrepressible. Once, he spied a beehive in a tree. Normally he would have shimmied up to investigate. But his arms were in casts: both wrists had been broken after he launched himself from a swing set. Undeterred, he hunted for a long stick, grasped it as best he could, and leapt up to poke the hive, breaking it apart. Bees poured forth from their ruined home and swarmed. So many stingers left their poison that his limbs swelled to twice their size, forcing doctors to cut off his casts.

Yet his inquisitiveness and fearlessness would never seriously harm him, and exploring nature brought him unmatched happiness. In this, he took after his parents. Family vacations were invariably spent in the West's majestic outdoor settings, where Milton Senior gloried in stretches of uninterrupted time with his kids. On family hikes Milt would run ahead of everyone, ever impatient to see around the next bend. He also fished in rivers and streams, usually catching enough for the family's supper. His father seldom joined him: he wasn't a sportsman, though he gratefully ate what his son caught.

Milt's earliest instruction in outdoor life came from his maternal grandparents. The Critchetts lived in Banning, California, in a two-room cabin built amid sycamores, beside a stream that ran under creek alders. Milt spent Easter and summer visits in the surrounding countryside. On hikes to waterfalls or abandoned mine shafts his grandpa taught him how to shoot a .22 rifle and hunt small game. "I was a holy terror to all the wild creatures, especially rabbits," Milt later reminisced. "I left song birds alone because my grandparents taught me not to kill them, but I did sometimes shoot up the poor lizard clan." The biggest trouble he ever got in came from throwing rocks through the tarpaper of the outdoor latrine. "My poor grandfather didn't spank me," he said, "but he made me wish that I had been more thoughtful and less destructive."

Milt's affinity for fishing was shared by neither grandparents nor parents. At six he constantly begged to go to area piers to observe fishermen and try his hand with rudimentary gear. Even an inexperienced "snagger" could manage a steady catch of small herring, horse sardines or jack-smelt. In *Tales of The Golden Years Of California Fishing*, Ed Ries describes what it was like to catch the fishing bug at Santa Monica. "Oblivious to dead bait, bird droppings, and splinters, I crouched or lay full length at the edge of the pier deck, tending my handline," he wrote. "Fishing ceased at nightfall, eight or ten hours later," he added. "Tired and famished, I toted my flour sack of perch up to the trolley

9

stop. To prevent any offense to other passengers, the conductor usually made me and my odorous sack of fish ride in the windy vestibule."

At seven, Milt would stand in the pier's bait-and-tackle store among stacked boxes of fishhooks, bundles of bamboo poles, and a large wooden barrel filled with anchovies. If the shop was busy he perused rental rods; or spools of linen line; or feather lures. If the clerk was idle Milt questioned him relentlessly. Outside, he watched to see who caught fish most successfully and pressed strangers for tips. His youth, earnestness, and enthusiasm helped him to charm anglers out of their best secrets, and it wasn't long before he was in the vestibule of the streetcar clutching his own sack of hard won fishes.

Milt spent the rest of his non-school hours playing with classmates and neighbors. He struggled to control his emotions in sports, but could always take solace in the outdoors. "Golly, there was always some newly discovered family of gophers or lizards roaming free in the big lot," he recalled. His own backyard was "a land in itself," where a boy could spend hours on "gang wars, fish graves, boxing matches, Easter-egg hunts, exploding firecrackers, bird shootings, window breaking, rock fights, kick the can, cops and robbers, hide and seek, statue, tag, kick-the-ball, frog tubs, pollywogs, wood piles." There were also the civilizing parts of middle-class childhood: piano lessons, Sunday school, chores.

On Milt's seventh birthday he got his first bicycle. That October he listened as the Chicago Cubs blew an eight run 7th inning lead to lose game 4 of the 1929 World Series. Sitting by the family radio again weeks later, he couldn't know the import of news that neither Milton Senior nor Ruth could fully grasp themselves. On Tuesday, October 29, 1929, there was a crash on the New York Stock Exchange. Harder times than any they had known lay ahead.

Three

THE DEPRESSION YEARS IN CALIFORNIA

As the Wall Street crash ravaged the Eastern economy, Californians were hopeful that distance, a productive agricultural sector, and regional institutions like the San Francisco-based Bank of America would provide a buffer. This hope ill-served Milton Senior. As 1929 drew to a close he grew frustrated with the Robert E. McKee construction company: promised bonuses didn't materialize and subcontractors faced long delays getting paid. Upset that men for whom he felt responsible weren't receiving their money, he resigned early in 1930. Underestimating the economic crisis, he then borrowed money to start his own construction company at perhaps the worst moment in American history to do so.

It didn't matter how diligently he prospected for clients: no one was building anything new. As weeks passed without work he recast himself as a craftsman-inventor, tinkering on an early version of an air-conditioning unit. The prototype made for a more pleasant summer on Stearns Drive but generated little income. As their savings shrank Milton Senior and Ruth did their best to keep their troubles from the children, who thrilled at extra time with their father. One day he drove them to a small airfield that would become LAX, explaining how important it would be to the region. Another time the family toured venues being readied for the 1932 Olympics.

The election that fall pitted Herbert Hoover, who the Shedds supported, against Franklin D. Roosevelt, the candidate many of their neighbors preferred. Ruth was a precinct captain. The Stearns Drive house was a polling place. Life still seemed mostly familiar to the kids. Father left the house every morning in search of work. Mother helped organize clothing drives for needy families. Money was tight, but there was enough for the children to put a dime each in the collection basket at Sunday school. And when Milt made a special request, as when he begged to join a local Boy Scouts troop, his mother would do her best to stretch the household budget a little farther, often assuring, "We'll find a way."

But the illusion of normalcy could only last so long. Unable to stretch the budget any more, Ruth quietly cancelled the kids' piano lessons. As construction continued to slump there were harder sacrifices, like the fantail pigeons that Milt raised as a hobby. The backyard birds were known to the family by name. Ruthie burst into tears one night when she realized that they had eaten George, her favorite of the flock, for dinner.

There was no money to pay Maria, who had become a member of the family. Ruth told her that she would always have a room in their home, food at their table, and a job if the hard times passed. She chose to stay, cooking meals, seeking help writing letters to her relatives, and walking to Catholic mass each morning. She couldn't help but notice the growing anxiety of Milton Senior and Ruth, and finally learned about a seemingly unresolvable financial emergency that marked the family's moment of greatest need. A devout parishioner, she had a close relationship with her priest and went to ask if he would lend the Shedds $200. The priest was skeptical that a family of Christian Scientists was deserving of Catholic charity. Ferociously loyal, Maria upbraided him, insisting that her household was as deserving as any. She returned home with a cash loan that carried the Shedds through their hardest weeks.

Milt did his best to contribute. One of his earliest jobs was hawking copies of *Liberty*, a general interest weekly magazine that sold for five cents. Later, he hired himself out mowing neighborhood lawns. He even did odd jobs for pay, though he had a knack for escaping unpaid chores. When truckloads of surplus construction material were dumped onto the driveway Milt and Irving were supposed to stack them in the backyard, but Milt so dominated his kid brother that he forced him to do it.

As Milt grew older, his greatest contribution to the family quickly became what he caught. He had started with the most basic gear: a used hand line, a cheap hook, and bait scrounged off pier boards. A rod and reel improved his catch. With practice, a few hours might yield a gunny sack half-filled with perch. But better anglers were scoring bonito. So Milt and others like him worked at catching bigger, *tastier* fish, until they could bag enough to sell their catch, update their equipment, and compete with the most capable pier-fishermen.

Access to deep water was a relatively new phenomenon in the state. The first municipal piers were built in the early 1900s. Those modest plank walks went no farther into the ocean than a man could swim. But merely getting beyond the surf, above pilings that gave cover to fish, was enough to make saltwater angling a mass phenomenon. Some days in the 1920s piers were so crowded that fishermen in suits, vests, and hats lined up shoulder-to-shoulder, frequently crossing their lines.

Entrepreneurs noticed. They bet that men jostling for spots a few dozen yards offshore would pay to fish in even deeper water. Hiring out small boats was prohibitively expensive for most pier fishermen. But what if old sailing ships that went out of service with the rise of steam could be repurposed into stationary platforms a couple miles offshore? That was the thought of Charles Arnold, who bought The Star of Scotland, a retired windjammer that he anchored off Santa Monica. The vessel was the talk of pier fisher-men, who admired it at twilight, its four masts and sails silhouetted by the setting sun.

Advertisements began to appear in local newspapers circa 1930: $1-per-day fares to fish on the 350-foot barge. Milt would watch anglers depart on water taxis that ran out to it throughout the morning, and see the same men return in the afternoon with more fishes than they could carry, including spe-cies that simply couldn't be caught from the pier. Now he would not be satis-fied until he could plumb the depths for those better fishes. He set his sights on becoming a barge fisherman.

Southern California's abundance of calm waters allowed many competing barges to operate off the coast. Milt and his contemporaries could get two miles offshore for as little as 75 cents. According to *Fishing Barges of California*, some men fished for even less by taking the last water taxi of the day to the Star of Scotland—25 cents bought permission to stay aboard all night. A six-booth restaurant served them dinner: the menu noted that the chef would cook any fish that they had caught for forty cents, a price that included bread, butter, coffee, and potatoes. Hunger satisfied, a man might play ping pong, fish into the wee hours beneath lights strung from the bowsprit, nap in a bunk, and rise at 5 a.m. for the first boat to shore.

Milt's parents would not approve an overnight outing no matter the savings. Rumor had it that some barges doubled as gambling dens in the wee hours. So he focused on saving a dollar for full fare during daylight hours, when Mrs. Arnold, the wife of the captain, took tickets. He likely started out catching mackerel, a common barge fish, and quickly got an angling education: Giant black seabass, now all but gone from Southern California, were regularly taken. Barracuda could be hooked using a feather jig; live bait dramatically improved the odds of landing prizes like yellowtail or white seabass. And halibut could be taken on hand-lines long enough to reach the sea bottom. Many amateur anglers were selling a portion of their catch. A determined barge fisherman could snag 30 halibut per day, as if Mother Nature had arranged years of bounty to offset dire times onshore.

Soon Milt was a "kid commercial," a youngster who financed his own fishing and made a small profit. His time outside school was spent preparing his equipment and getting to the pier, an easier task once his indulgent sister got a driver's license.

Milt would ask neighbors if they wanted to place an order; get to Santa Monica or Long Beach; earn barge fare by working for a couple hours on a boat that gathered bait fish; and spend the rest of the day on his small-time operation, trying his best to fill whatever orders he had taken for specific fishes. He could sell a barracuda for 25 cents. Halibut fetched three times that. Anything extra would help to feed his family. On good nights, the Shedds ate tuna, halibut, or seabass, burying surplus mackerel in the yard where it helped the plants to grow. Other nights, the Shedds ate the mackerel, finding it less offensive after Maria figured out that frying it with bacon morsels softened its flavor.

Eventually, Milt used some of his earnings to put a down payment on a refrigerator so that the family could save the best fish that he brought home for multiple meals. With the rise of federally funded public works projects, Milt Senior finally started to find construction jobs that paid a steady salary. While the loan from Maria's priest had long since been repaid, he continued to bear the burden of other debt he had taken on, especially after three of Milt's grandparents and one uncle died in short order, requiring multiple trips back to El Paso. Those stresses aside, life for the Shedds regained a semblance of normality. Milton Senior worked long hours and traveled often. Milt began to play competitive tennis. As a freshman at Fairfax High School he earned above average grades, played football in the fall, and excelled on the pitcher's mound that spring.

In 1938, Ruthie graduated high school and her parents were able to purchase a sweater that she earned for exceptional marks. For the Shedds, that signified the end of the Depression. Ruthie enrolled the following February at UCLA, where tuition was $35 per semester. She commuted, joined a Christian Science Club, and pledged Alpha Delta Gamma. Milt, who had become a star pitcher, graduated from high school in 1940. He caught a marlin that summer off San Diego and followed his sister to UCLA, where he planned to study business, play sports, and pass four years before facing adulthood. Once again, world events would upend the future he imagined.

Four

Young Love at UCLA

Peggie Rich was increasingly annoyed as she waited and waited in the frat house den. A Latin major who lived with her divorced mother to save money, she looked on as her sorority sisters danced with their dates. They all seemed to be having fun. Her date lived right there in the frat house. But he had yet to arrive.

The match had been made weeks earlier during a mothers' brunch at Alpha Delta Gamma. Peggie's mother had hit it off with Mrs. Ruth Shedd, the mother of her sorority sister. Both mothers belonged to the Christian Science church and decided their children, Milt and Peggie, ought to meet. The coming social with Phi Kappa Sigma struck them as the perfect opportunity. As Peggie waited, she brooded on agreeing to attend with this increasingly tardy boy. Where could he be?

Milt burst in moments later, having rushed straight from a football practice that let out late. He was a mess: sweaty, winded, and bleeding from a cut on his forehead that was only half-covered by a hastily applied bandage. Oblivious to Peggie's displeasure, he didn't apologize for being tardy. He was an enthusiastic, intense conversation partner: friendly, earnest, and a bit overwhelming in a loud room half-shouting to be heard.

When someone played The Glenn Miller Orchestra's hit, The Chattanooga Choo Choo, he danced rambunctiously, forgetful of his size and strength. Prevailing on Peggie to join him in its signature steps, he watched her gamely attempt a dance she didn't know, then stopped her mid-song to explain that it was all wrong—the steps called for more of this and less of that. Peggie was confounded. Her date seemed to enjoy her company and she sensed that he had a good heart, despite it all. But he was so uncouth! As the night ended Peggie wasn't sorry. She decided that she had not enjoyed their date.

That autumn of 1941, UCLA was no more than a half-dozen buildings clustered near a fledgling Westwood Village. Its leaders knew that L.A. would grow and assumed UCLA would mature slowly alongside it. In this way, they resembled its freshmen students: 17-and-18-year-olds expecting to ease into maturity over four predictable years of lectures, football games, and prom dates.

As a freshman back in 1940, Milt couldn't begin to fathom all that would transpire before he got his diploma. He was rushing Phi Kappa Sigma, as his father had done decades prior. Its brothers, known on campus for their annual Hawaii-themed party, were described in a yearbook as "play time boys with plenty of date luncheons and dinners." According to the same description, "crew men predominate... but the army places a close second." Milt had joined the ROTC at his father's urging. When he wasn't drilling or at athletic practice he spent his time at the frat house horsing around. The brothers would challenge one another to contests trading swats on the behind with wooden paddles. Hyper-competitive in all things, Milt would relish squaring off against bigger, older boys and thwacking them with all his might. Peers soon knew that he never backed down.

1940 was a fine year to be at UCLA. On November 29, the day before the big football game against USC, much of the student body assembled in Royce Hall where they rang a victory bell 60 times and joined in chants and yells. That night, a local radio station broadcast the UCLA fight song to all of Los Angeles. The next morning, *The Daily Bruin* pleaded, "It is imperative that the rooters bring any megaphones they have at home to the game because of a shortage." That afternoon, 70,000 fans assembled in the Coliseum to see the game. Most of the Bruin faithful had fun despite the final outcome.

On December 4, 1940, the student newspaper teased an upcoming dance. It was the talk of campus, receiving far greater prominence than the previous day's guest lecture by Dr. Frederick Libber, founder of the National Council for the Prevention Of War. "We are too late," he told his audience. "Britain cannot win even with our help." The headline: "Libber says US must learn to live with Hitler." UCLA's men took notice that spring, when the service exemption that kept college students out of any draft expired. But even then, many saw events in Europe, Africa, and Asia as abstractions: less real than Los Angeles sunshine, frat house socials, and smiling coeds.

Happily settled on campus, Milt made the baseball team that spring, displaying enough talent to pitch on the varsity roster as a freshman.

The following autumn, he made the football squad, and soon after he met Peggie at that fraternity exchange. He had never been more enamored. Perceiving their introduction as a success, he hoped to run into her on campus for weeks afterward. On the quad, he would search eagerly for her in crowds. The faces of the other girls no longer seemed as pretty. Sometimes he would get lucky and see her. She would be leaving class or waiting at the bus stop or walking on Le Conte Avenue toward Westwood Village. He always said hello.

And Peggie began to soften. After a few conversations, she liked him more than she had that first night, when he had danced the Chattanooga Choo Choo too fast. He would tease her about her studiousness, saying that he could always rely on finding her in the library doing Latin homework. She understood it was his way of flirting. Come December, Milt still hadn't been out alone with Peggie. But she finally agreed to a date.

Then the whole world changed.

"On December 7, 1941, the sky over UCLA was bright blue and the air spring-like," an official university history recounts. "Because it was a Sunday, the campus was largely deserted, the only signs of life being a couple bicycle riders, a family with children romping on the lawn, and a handful of students trudging toward the library. A radio news flash at 11:31 am brought little immediate reaction on campus. On Monday morning, however, students and faculty overflowed Royce Hall Auditorium to hear, via radio, Franklin D. Roosevelt's address to Congress asking for a declaration of war against Japan."

UCLA staff quickly rigged air raid sirens and prepared for the worst. As the nation transitioned to war-footing unfamiliar guest lecturers were invited to speak about the situation abroad. There were still dances. But students would as often socialize at scrap drives. The football team still played USC, its crosstown rival, but students at the two schools also competed to see who could sell more war bonds. On exam days, paper shortages meant blue books were scarce. The dining hall instituted "meatless Tuesdays" to conserve protein. No one could remember Sunday services so well-attended.

The fear that gripped Angelenos after Pearl Harbor is largely forgotten. It peaked on February 25, 1942, when Western Defense Command reported that enemy planes had been spotted over the city. The military went on high alert and began firing hundreds of anti-aircraft shells into the dark as searchlights swept the empty sky. "For that hour, as sirens wailed and yellow tracer bullets pierced the blackness, and anti-aircraft barrages exploded overhead in fiery orange bursts of shrapnel, and paths of light crisscrossed overhead in search of enemy aircraft, Los Angeles enjoyed a make-believe version, a Hollywood version, of the London blitz," Kevin Starr writes in *Embattled Dreams*, his history of wartime California.

In that Los Angeles, Milt Shedd courted Peggie Rich. On their first formal date, the couple drove to a movie in a borrowed car, making the return trip without headlights to observe a blackout. That spring, as Milt practiced his pitching, he would take breaks beside the infield to have long talks with Peggie. They wrote notes back and forth, too. Milt could be brief and sweet, but would sometimes fill pages with detailed thoughts and arguments about world events or philosophy, exasperating Peggie. He usually apologized for getting carried away.

Peggie remembers how surprised some of her friends were when they heard that she was dating Milt. They had known him in high school, when he had never shown any interest in girls, just sports and fishing. But Peggie found Milt very handsome. And it was growing easier for her to see past his flaws to core values and sensibilities that they actually shared.

As the couple began their junior year, Marines were landing on Guadalcanal, Nazis were preparing to attack Stalingrad, and Rommel was undefeated in Egypt. Milt knew that he would be sent to war. But he was in love for the first time. Each morning, he awoke amid friends in gorgeous weather. His steady girlfriend was named UCLA's homecoming queen. They were both class officers, popular in the Greek system and widely liked. Come spring, he would be the star pitcher on the baseball team and Peggie would be on the sideline cheering him on. Had any young man better cause for living in the moment?

Now Peggie went happily to the frat. She arrived with her sorority sisters, delighting the boys by bringing food and getting nowhere urging them to reupholster the sofa. A photograph taken that year shows the couple playing ping-pong as a team. In another, they are gathered for a meeting to plan prom. Milt was assistant chairman of the committee. In a later photo he is smiling at the dance beside Peggie. He wore his navy blue ROTC jacket with brass buttons. The few boys who didn't have uniforms wore tuxedos, the less fashionable choice that year. Everyone danced to Freddy Martin, the band leader and tenor saxophonist, who played long past midnight.

It would be Milt and Peggie's first and last school formal together. That spring he was ordered to report for officer training in Fort Benning, Georgia. Suddenly, he had no more time. His father, who anticipated his thoughts, told him that it would be unfair to marry Peggie only to depart for war perhaps never to return. Seldom, if ever, had Milt gone against his father's wishes. At the same time, he was a stubborn young man and determined to do what he deemed right. He proposed.

As Peggie remembers it,

> "We didn't have a long time to decide anything, because we were just two kids having a good time in college, studying and doing what we were supposed to be doing. And then the world comes along and knocks everything to smithereens. It was, 'Are you going to marry him or are you not going to marry him,' because he was already there. I don't know what made me fall in love, because I sure didn't like him the night that I met him. But I really got to enjoy his company. One day we sat down on a park bench and talked about the future. He always knew what he wanted. He said, 'I have a brother and a sister and I want to have three kids.' I said, 'I'm an only child, two might be okay.' But he wanted three kids. He was a pistol, I'll tell you."

Engaged before basic training, they planned to marry that September. Milt gave everyone a scare when his drive back from Georgia took a couple of days longer than expected, but arrived in time for the wedding at St. Albans church on the UCLA campus.

Everyone walked to Alpha Gamma Delta for the reception. The couple took the weekend to honeymoon in Santa Monica, then packed their things and moved to Camp White in Medford, Oregon.

All nearby houses were occupied, so the newlyweds rented an extra room from an old schoolteacher. She was tough on the young couple, complaining that they didn't keep the kitchen neat enough and insisting that they could only have one shower each per week. Milt said he would give his shower to Peggie. The landlady insisted they would lose it if he didn't take the shower himself.

They lived in Oregon for five months. Milt was on base all day. Peggie worked for the gas board, doling out ration tickets so that soldiers could get their share of fuel. Among her worst memories was a weekend hunting trip they took to get food for the winter. "He would shoot the ducks and I would pick them up," she remembers. "That was fine. But it was cold. Snow all over the place. He kept shooting. And I kept retrieving. And then it got darker and darker, and colder and colder. He was dressed in his full uniform with the boots and everything. I had tennis shoes on." When they camped that night she nearly froze. "So he got the engine going in the car, and it quit running. The car wouldn't go anymore. He still thought that it was the best hunting trip—he loved it up there, said that when the war ended we ought to go live there. I thought it was one of the worst times that we ever had together."

Milt hung the pheasants, ducks and geese in his landlady's garage, where they would keep through the winter months. "She used to get so mad, that little lady," Peggie said. "She couldn't understand it even though she was stuck with them." No matter. Milt looked forward to a winter with the birds there anytime they wanted something to eat. And he was eager for his next months on base too. Increasingly enamored of flying, he had put in for a transfer to the Army Air Corps, where he hoped to become a fighter pilot. He was surprised to be called before a general who got upset that a man wanted to leave his command. In a fit of pique, the general decided Milt would be a replacement officer for an infantry regiment at the front.

Milt was suddenly gone.

Five

War

"**I**'m somewhere near the middle of the blue-bluest ocean I've ever seen. We are having a wonderfully good time!" So began the first of many wartime letters that Milt sent via Army mail to his wife. "What amazes me most is the albatross," he marveled. "Our ship is not slow, yet these graceful creatures circle us for hours and rarely do you see one so much as flap its wings. They swoop and sail without a bit of effort, landing occasionally to pick up a piece of garbage; then with one flap they glide back into position behind our stern."

Other soldiers were seasick. Torpedo drills were a daily reminder of the threat from submarines. Fighting lay ahead. But before Milt was assigned to a combat unit, faced hostile fire, or flew in spotter planes over enemy territory; before he killed an enemy soldier, saw the death of a man under his command, or crept through jungle foliage on reconnaissance missions, he left his shared quarters, stood at the rail of a transport ship, and delighted in what he saw. "After the men have bedded down," he explained, "the only sounds audible are the splashing of the waves against the side of the ship and the dull, heavy throbbing of the ship engines." Passing clouds were "fine-textured lace," and appeared "unbelievably white in the moonlight." He saw flying fish everyday but observed, "we are not yet in what I'd call good fishing waters."

Milt was bound for an island 750 miles east of Australia, where he would await orders as a replacement officer. Put another way, he would be subbing for a man who had been killed, wounded, or felled by tropical disease. But he scarcely let on. "I've been waiting to get into a good rough sea, and this looks like it!" he wrote when he was nearly ashore during Easter Week of 1944. Soon after disembarking a chance to hunt and fish presented itself. "For the past five days I've been exploring… this place is a paradise for a fellow like myself," he declared. "I've had a marvelous time–so far."

Milt would spend two weeks on New Caledonia. He slept in a tent eight-feet high at the center, using a barracks bag as a pillow and a steel helmet as a wash basin. Latrines were 50 yards away, the mess hall 150 yards farther, and the beach a mile more. "All afternoon I swam in the clearest saltwater," he wrote. "The sand is white and fine but doesn't cloud up the water… it was easily 20 feet deep; yet I could see the bottom and small fish all around." He and a friend found a rowboat and explored a small atoll two miles from shore. "The coral here is of many colors and very beautiful," he wrote. "Strange plants, fish and sea life are a constant." He noted sea snakes and giant turtles. "Before long I'll have a good tan, and even better, I'll be a fairly good swim-mer," he predicted. "I didn't believe this life of ease was going to last for long; yet it continues."

When next at sea, he spent his watch searching the water for sharks. As is-lands became visible he would ask their names. "These are places I read about during the past two years," he wrote. A week later, he disembarked on "the swampiest and boggiest place I've ever seen."

He was on Guadalcanal.

He camped on the beach, gathered sea shells for Peggie, and wrote about a crocodile hunt that he embarked on after spotting the creature in the ocean. He and a friend borrowed a canoe so unstable that it flipped over twice as they gave chase. "This lack of stability worried me no end as I had seen 3 or 4 large sharks that same day within 100 yards of shore," Milt wrote. "But foolishly or courageously I stripped myself of all clothes but my shorts, and still carrying my rifle and 15 rounds we again attempted to put out to sea."

His travelogue tone broke only after he got word that his next stop would be an island with fighting. "I'm in much the same position as the 'Chosen' Aztec Youth in the days of very old Mexico when the Aztec civilization was at its height," he wrote. "I know it all must end sometime." His destination was Bougainville, Solomon Islands, where he would take command of enlisted men. He had been preparing to keep his wits about him even as others lost theirs, advice he cribbed from Rudyard Kipling. And he would lead better, he thought, if he knew the history of his new outfit, so he asked the men around him to share their stories.

They were quite different from his own.

When President Roosevelt and Congress declared war on Japan, the 164th Infantry Regiment of North Dakota had last seen action in The Great War. Almost no veterans remained. During the 1930s, when most of its enlisted men joined, national guard companies were part of peacetime life in prairie towns. On signing up, a 17-year-old would gain the respect of his elders, a sharp dress-uniform, and better odds of convincing the local saloonkeeper to look past his age if he ordered a beer. Later, he would stand a better chance of winning local office.

During the Depression years, pay was another compelling reason to join. Young North Dakotans "hired out with threshing crews at harvest time, found jobs, quit school and sometimes rode the rails to find work," Terry Shoptaugh wrote in *They Were Ready*, a chronicle of the regiment. Why not earn a dollar for an afternoon of marches or $15 at summer training camp? The possibility of war seemed remote. Machine-gunners didn't even get ammunition for practice until 1939. But the very next year the regiment was called up for 12 months of training. Their towns organized sendoffs that portended a longer absence. "Dances were held, mayors gave speeches, choirs sang, and churches held service," Shoptaugh wrote. "Veterans of the First World War and members of the local American Legions acted as honor guards as the companies marched to the nearest train stations." They were headed farther from home than most had ever been.

And Camp Claiborne, Louisiana, had more mosquitoes, chiggers, and ticks than they had ever seen. There were alligators in the water where they trained, too. Bayou life was bearable mostly because their year of active duty would soon be over. They felt misled and resentful when Congress extended their service by 18 months. Then came Pearl Harbor. Overnight, the regiment was ordered to San Francisco—they boarded trains expecting to help repel a Japanese invasion.

At UCLA, Milt was enjoying his autumn semester as the 164th passed beneath the Golden Gate Bridge, crossed the Pacific and deposited its men on New Caledonia for orientation. By that time, Japan had seized control of Korea, Manchuria, Guam, the Philippines, French Indochina, Singapore, the Dutch East Indies, Siam, Burma, parts of New Guinea, and the Solomon Islands. The U.S. hoped to gain a foothold on Guadalcanal, where Marines seized a partially completed airfield, dying in great numbers.

The Army reinforced them with the North Dakota farm boys, who waded ashore on October 13, 1942, just as Japanese warships started shelling. Then enemy bombers appeared overhead. The new troops sought cover, each grappling in real time with the terror of arbitrary death. That first air-raid killed one farm boy, who was buried in the Marine cemetery by comrades who had known him since childhood. Another onslaught began after midnight: ships spent hours bombarding U.S. positions with shells. Forty-one Americans were killed.

The new troops were ordered to the perimeter the next day. "The Thing had not yet infected them," Marine Samuel Baglien later wrote. "War was still a lark. Their faces were heavy with flesh, their ribs padded, their eyes innocent." Yet they held the line 11 days later during an attack, even as "Japanese dead piled up against the wire and pressed a section of it to the ground."

The next night, another attack killed 35 men from the regiment. The survivors suffered more casualties pursuing the enemy: they charged over hills with Japanese machine guns trained on their crests; while crouching behind jungle foliage, grenades sent shrapnel into their guts and skulls. Others suffered from mosquito-borne disease, dysentery, heat stroke, and nervous breakdown. That autumn, "three days of combat almost doubled the casualties of the regiment," Shoptaugh wrote, putting total losses at 117 men killed, 208 men wounded, and 325 men evacuated. With half of its officers gone and its forces depleted, the 164th was brought into reserve. In victory, 7,100 Americans died on Guadalcanal.

The North Dakotans spent most of 1943 on Fiji, a peaceful island. Men already infected with malaria collapsed as jaundice and fever gripped them. As the worst cases were sent home the regiment shrunk to less than half its original force. Those who remained enjoyed the presence of American nurses, native women, USO shows, and plentiful liquor. Officers mostly overlooked drunken misbehavior, knowing that the men had fought hard, and that they would be ordered to do so again after what turned out to be 11 months of downtime.

By November 1943, while Milt and Peggie were enjoying their brief time as newlyweds in Oregon, the remaining North Dakotans were ordered to Bougainville, the biggest of the Solomon Islands. It stretched 130 miles, Shoptaugh wrote, with "a central spine of high, rugged mountains, a tropical rain forest, and a shallow, rapidly running river that ended in a swamp." They waded ashore on Christmas Day 1943. Marines had already fortified a perimeter and seized strategic hills.

Seventeen men from the regiment were soon killed in scattered fighting, but most were able to avoid enemy fire until March 8, 1944, when four Japanese battalions charged the American perimeter. Once again, soldiers from the 164th helped repel the attack and generals judged that, having done so, they should give chase. The North Dakotans climbed rugged hills, fought day and night, and struggled to get their wounded back to base, for the jungle teemed with snipers. In defeat, the Japanese refused to surrender: infantrymen had to risk stalking them through the jungle to kill them in small groups.

Milt arrived on Bougainville during a lull in the fighting. His tent stood near the top of a steep hill with a good view of the terrain. At its summit, a hundred-foot tree offered a single, sturdy-looking vine that dangled from a high branch. "We take the end and walk up the hill," he wrote on May 18. "Then we swing down. At the far side of the arc we are at least thirty to forty feet above the ground. What fun playing Tarzan." He would look down at the jungle, a seemingly tranquil carpet of light and dark greens, and reassure Peggie of his safety. "The Japs aren't interested in getting killed, so they stay away," he reported. He went on to reflect on how lucky he was to arrive on the island in mild weather. "The sun is shining brightly but there is a cool breeze," he wrote. "The sky is very blue, and there are many beautiful butterflies fluttering about."

The regiment spent the last days of May preparing for imminent hostilities. Milt would participate as a second lieutenant, but also as an erstwhile collegian who had faced nothing more fearsome than an opposing batter standing athwart home plate. He posed questions during lectures and sought tips from combat veterans. On patrols, he resolved to enforce strict order: staying at least five yards apart; keeping to the edges of trails; proceeding as if booby traps might be hidden at any point; tolerating neither chatter nor cigarette smoking.

His ability to safeguard the lives of others was tested even before he ventured near the enemy. On June 3, 1944, he took a trip to a beach inside the American perimeter. He had been diligently practicing his swimming, knowing it might come in handy if a transport boat was hit by a torpedo or a swiftly moving river had to be crossed. That day, amid heavy surf and rip currents, "I ventured out a little too far," he wrote, "and found myself in a river-like current taking me out to sea. I wasn't a bit scared as I had complete confidence in my ability to get to shore no matter how far out I was carried." But two others were also swept out to sea. Both were struggling to stay afloat. "We were 200 yards or more out and the current wasn't slackening," Milt wrote. "I didn't want two drowning men on my hands. So I told the stronger looking fellow to go in if he thought he could make it. I was glad that he left as he seemed quite jittery and I knew I couldn't take care of three of us."

Milt turned to the remaining man and asked his name. "Bob was in a bad way, completely exhausted and scared to death," he recounted. "I was afraid that he would drown us both." Bob had been riding an inflated mattress cover when a wave knocked him into the surf. He was from Idaho, didn't know how to swim, and was helpless as the rip current took him. "We must have been 500 yards out," Milt wrote. "I was more than a little uneasy. I knew if I left him I could save myself, but at the same time I figured I could go on a while longer."

Eventually Bob calmed down enough to listen. "I told him to put his right arm around my waist—I kept him afloat," Milt wrote. "He kept pushing me under. I tried to get him to float by himself but he sank like a log. I let him flounder by himself for a minute while I floated on my back and caught my breath and rested… I thought about leaving him, especially when he got excited and grabby." Although tiring, Milt started dragging him slowly back shoreward. "The rising swells helped," he wrote. "Finally I saw a big wave come in and tried to ride it with him, but we knocked together something awful. When I saw another big wave I told him we'd try to ride it in separately. I thought it would finish me."

"It swirled, tumbled, tossed and dashed me. I had taken a good breath and didn't try to fight. Then I could touch bottom and keep my nose out of the water. I never expected to see Bob again." But he was just 30 yards back.

"The plucky devil was shouting 'Help! Help! Help!' for all he was worth. I was just about pooped, so I stood there for about 20 seconds. After taking a few big puffs I started after him," Milt wrote. "The next wave plus a few kicks put us where we could touch bottom. When he caught his breath he said, 'Thanks, golly thanks a lot for saving my life.' I told him he would've drowned us both had he not calmed down. At Santa Monica, I'd have stayed around for handshakes and the camera man. But out here what I did was a small thing compared to what others have done, although it was a big thing for me. Lieutenant Ross said I almost deserved a medal. After I had pulled the kid out of the ocean I jumped in the truck without sticking around for people to say nice things. But I left with a good feeling."

Milt's first patrol began early the next morning. The jungle was quiet save for honey bees and rotting tree branches that fell noisily through the canopy. "I saw lots of Japs, all dead and pretty well rotted away," he wrote. "I wasn't scared but tingly, the same sensation I have when I am tracking down a buck or waiting for a big goose to fly overhead." On a second patrol he buried a dead Japanese soldier. "You don't think of them as humans," he observed, "so the bodies don't bother me." He added, "I guess they all look at us the same way."

As Milt led uneventful patrols with the 164th their Allies in Europe were launching the most massive amphibious invasion in history. On June 6, 1944, more than 160,000 troops landed on heavily fortified beaches in Normandy,

supported by 13,000 planes and 5,000 ships. More than 9,000 Allied soldiers were killed and 100,000 began fighting their way through France in an offensive that wouldn't end until Germany's unconditional surrender. "At last the invasion is on," Milt wrote.

On Bougainville, the American perimeter remained secure. After the stress of a long patrol, Milt could go back to his tent, where tropical birds perched in nearby trees and jungle critters helped him to unwind. "Have just been playing with a little green lizard, trying to feed him bugs, but poor fellow, he was too scared to eat," Milt wrote, calling him "one of my many friends who share this tent with me—I see them all the time, scooting across the canvas ceiling, exploring my clothes, crawling in and out of my shoes." They were poor substitutes for Phantom X, the beloved pet dog that he left at home. "I wanted to make one my personal friend, so I caught him; but I'm too big; he doesn't like me; so I let him go," Milt explained. "He is going back now to tell his buddies about the terrible giant and his capture and escape. He'll be a hero in Lizardville."

Milt spent the rest of June and July delivering lectures, censoring mail, and tending a vegetable garden. "Although Lt. Ross is the public relations officer, I will write up items on some of my men for their hometown newspapers," he wrote. "The boys deserve to read about themselves." He sought help from Peggie, photographing the men, sending her the film, and getting prints by return mail. Handing them out seemed to help morale.

"Today has been an easy day," he wrote on June 20, 1944. He had gone in search of netting for the regiment's basketball hoops and noted in a proud letter home that his team had won 22 of 25 games. He also played softball with officers and acted as an umpire in games for the enlisted men. Another day he watched an organized boxing match. "The crowd hollered for blood and became angry and felt cheated unless the fighters mixed it rough and hurt one another," he told Peggie. "I get all excited myself but in every fight there must be a loser and a boy that gets hurt a little more; so I don't believe I'll ever become much of a fight fan. The bloodthirsty fans are usually those that couldn't beat their way out of a wet paper bag and I don't care to put myself in their class."

Days later he wrote: "I killed my first two Japs."

At first, he didn't make much of it. "Just a matter of sneaking up on them," he wrote. "I threw four grenades right in the middle of the group." He cast the closeness of the combat as a stroke of luck rather than a peril or trauma. "I'm glad to do my fighting in this part of the world," he explained, for patrols pitted man against man more often than the machines that ruled in Europe. "You depend on your own ability to keep alive, as near as could be to the Indian fighting in the frontier days." But the nearness of the enemy soon made Milt feel as though something within him was harder than it had been. On another patrol, his platoon happened on Japanese soldiers as they bathed, then surreptitiously followed them back to a hidden camp. "I was the first man into their positions," he wrote. "I killed six at ranges from twenty yards to two yards with my tommy gun. One or two were wounded, but I had to take no chances. When I shot them I did not feel one way or the other about it. They might just as well have been tin cans or paper targets." He added, "I didn't believe I could be so unconcerned in doing such a thing. No, Dearest, I'll never go around killing people when I get home. But I am liable to be 'unconcerned' about something that might 'concern' someone else very much. I'm telling you these things so you will understand me better."

That August, the regiment got favorable news: Germany's defeat appeared to be assured. For Milt, a happy mood spurred reflections on his natural surroundings. Jungle trees "appear as tall as telephone polls with umbrellas of foliage stuck out at the top," he observed. "Others have the appearance of the towering heads of a mammoth giant whose hair is disheveled." He admired "the complicated lattice work of gently swaying vines," dubbing it beautiful yet mysterious, "as out of the darkness drifts the countless sounds of jungle chatter. The greatest violators of peace and quiet are Bill and Mary Cricket singing to one another. The atmosphere is something to enjoy."

In darker moods, he complained about commanding officers. After a patrol "to visit the scene of a slaughter with the intent to kill any surviving Nips and pick up intelligence," he wrote, "I was greeted by the battalion intelligence officer in a very inconsiderate manner. Before he asked if I had any casualties, what condition my men were in, or what information we had found, he began reprimanding me for turning in my report before he had received it… He wanted credit… Mind you, all my men had not even crossed the finish line."

A promotion helped to alleviate his frustration: he was made a 1st Lieutenant. He had coveted the rank, though it meant greater peril. Before departing on a subsequent patrol that he portrayed as not particularly dangerous in a letter home, he wrote Peggie a separate letter, dated August 15, 1944, that addressed the possibility of his death. Calling it "straight from the shoulder," he declared, "I expect you to accept it as fact and not to become emotional," as he would "pull no punches."

He continued:

"In the movies it is customary for the husband to write a letter to his wife and have his best friend keep it for him. Such letters are written as 'thanks for all you have done for me, and we did have such wonderful times together, etc.' You might call it the climax and conclusion to their great adventure, and its effect is that of a highly emotional stimulant. I'm writing a letter of somewhat this nature, but I'm sending it to you now.

It is hardly a letter that expects an answer. You will probably consider me mad. I need not mention the 'thanks for everything' as I've expressed my love for you in absolute terms many times. So this is more of an 'advice' message, and tells how I want you to 'behave for my sake.' Certainly you will not agree with me now (maybe you do—I hope you're practical minded in such matters and do agree) but I want you to agree should I meet my death.

I'd better explain that I have no intentions of being killed. Sure, it is possible. I'm writing about realities. But this kid is learning fast how to take care of himself. This all sounds rather melodramatic, doesn't it? I'll grant that my method of putting information across is subject to criticism. People may disagree with me but argument would not change my ideas. Actually I see nothing to argue about. What you do with this letter is your concern. If it frightens you, you can burn it up with much ado, but I'd much rather have you keep it as a joke that we can laugh about in later years, although even I don't consider this subject a joke now.

Well, so much for the introduction. Now for the body—a literary phrase, my dear, not me. In simple and few words, if I'm killed I do expect you to shed a few tears for me. It would take time for the effects to wear off, but you are not to wear 'a black mourning dress' for the rest of your life. I of course at that time would have little to say as to what you did. You undoubtedly would, I hope, forget me, to a great extent, in time, and find another person as you are very young. THAT IS WHAT I EXPECT AND WANT YOU TO DO. Anybody can weep and mourn about losing their mate, but you have character and will go on living a happy normal life. If I am unable to always work on my objective of making yours a perfect lifetime, I don't want the job left undone. I would be happy in Heaven or Hell to know that you had remarried and gone right on living and doing the things we planned. I'd expect you to forget me. That would be the natural thing for you to do.

Now for the conclusion.

Don't you dare get all excited at what I've written. Remember I have left my emotions out of writing this. You do the same when you read it. Now for a little emotion. My Dearest, I may be "too factual" but I do love you tremendously. I want and expect to go right on living our life together, but I want you to know how I feel if our plans don't follow through. We will laugh about this letter in two years or sooner, won't we, Sweetheart?

We sure will.

Nothing but love from your Milt.

Ps. I am not writing this letter because my next 10 days will be fraught with danger and hazard, but because I had time and a typewriter handy. I'll be perfectly safe all the time I'm out.

Bye bye. "

Predictably, he had been far from safe, writing upon his return:

"I'm so mad! I wrote you a long letter while under the very nose of the Nips—machine guns, mortars and artillery going full blast—and I lost it! It told all about my sneaking up on a Nip pill box for observation purposes... boy am I mad."

He still preferred action to inaction, as when he volunteered his exceptional eyesight to help guide a bomber strike. "I love flying," he wrote. "When we finished bombing my target, on which many planes dropped several tons, the lead plane in which I was flying had a secondary mission of bombing out a bridge, so we went on to do this job. Mission accomplished!" Another time he declared, as if complaining, "We'll be in the rear area for some time. They figure we have done our share for awhile."

He disliked the rear, for it meant composing lectures, teaching classes, and all manner of administrative drudgery. That September, however, his duties changed: due to his exceptional performance on patrols, he was transferred to regimental command headquarters, made reconnaissance officer, and given leadership of a platoon. He was charged with knowing where Japanese troops were and what they were doing. "I am pretty much on my own," he wrote, "deciding what training my men need, making up the schedule, etc. I eat at the colonels' mess. I sleep in good quarters. I always have transportation. I do not spend time doing guard work."

Once again, he had leapfrogged other men for the job. "There are many better qualified than I for this work who have fought through Guadalcanal and the campaign on this island," he explained. "Some are bound to be resentful. One can't blame them. That is life, especially army life... I have learned to keep quiet when it is wisest to do so, as I have learned how important it is not to affect people adversely." At first, the new reconnaissance group spent its days clearing sections of the jungle: the men would hack at towering trees and get a kick out of hollering "Timber!" as they crashed down. Their work site was across a stream that had to be forded each day and got treacherous in rain, but Milt preferred spending as much time as possible away from regimental headquarters. He felt that men assigned there weren't good soldiers or efficient workers as he had expected. "They are smoothies and backslappers," he grumbled. "I subordinate myself and inflate their egos, so I get along fine. But being quick to notice discrepancies I have unpleasant food for thought."

The morning of October 15, 1944, his platoon left on a five-day patrol, tasked with finding a route through the swamp to flank the enemy. "We each carried two canteens, a shelter half, one poncho, a square section of rubberized canvas used as a raincoat, and machetes," he wrote. "At night we built shacks out of banana leaves, slept on the shelter half as a floor and used the poncho as a blanket." After four days they confirmed that the swamp was impassable. Rather than hack back through the jungle, Milt decided that they should save time by floating themselves and their gear downstream toward base, though he had previously seen crocodiles in the river. To be safe they built rafts large enough to put one man on top as three others floated alongside. "I wanted a man up high where he could use his tommy gun in case the crocs or the Nips came after us," he explained. "We looked like Robinson Crusoes." The trip was uneventful until they rounded a bend: "The men on the raft that had just passed us yelled 'alligators,' dove off their raft and headed for shore. It was funny to see how excited they became. There went their equipment downstream and they were on the bank feeling helpless. I told them to swim to our raft as we could cover them. Two did as I suggested, but the other had already taken off down the bank to catch up with his raft. It was a sight seeing a grown man dashing madly through the jungle in only his shorts."

With monsoon season, Milt once again marveled at his surroundings. "I have never in my life seen so much rain," he wrote. "Every day I put my helmet outside for shaving water and it is filled." He used the time indoors to write his uncle a letter describing a patrol he had led:

"We had rested at our hidden perimeter point to reach the enemy when all would be in from their search for food and might be congregated in preparing their evening meal... They had lived here for months unmolested. They had no security! We could hear them chopping wood... I cautioned the men to be extremely quiet crossing the deep, steep gully only 70 yards from the nips. When nearly at the bottom I slipped on a wet clay band and landed on my ___. I sat there for what seemed like hours, but was only seconds, with my carbine trained on the facing bank above, listening. But the Nips kept right on chopping... "

Milt and his men eventually snuck up onto the river bank nearest the camp. The enemy lived in wooden shacks:

"It was quite a sensation to find yourself in a "field manual" situation. When I saw those Nips going about their business getting ready for supper I felt like I did when sighting down my first Buck. I appreciate all my hunting experiences and participation in athletics. It long ago taught me to control that run away feeling in my stomach. What to do! I lay and watched them for 5 minutes thinking about what course of action I should take."

They had trained for such a situation just days before.

"So we were all of the same mind. I guess proper training conditions a man to think in an orderly manner and he unconsciously follows a plan of systemized thinking when under stress. We couldn't be seen because of the dense vegetation, but neither did we have a good field of fire... We had to move farther down the forward slope to where the bank dropped away. The men moved forward individually, crawling sometimes in plain view of the enemy... and showed the results of good discipline and combat experience. They would do their firing only if detected, or on my signal, which would mean the throwing of grenades. I had collected 8 of them and all during this phase of the operation held one, pin pulled, in each hand."

It took them fifteen minutes to creep into the perfect positions. They lay in wait a bit longer as everyone picked out their targets, none farther than 40 yards away.

"I could see 3 nips sleeping in shack number one... A group of six was eating in shack number two, and two more chopping wood. Others would occasionally show themselves moving from one hut to another. There must have been nearly 25 or the better part of a platoon. I had cautioned the men to lay their magazines in front of them where they could get at them easily. I pointed at six Nips eating and then at the three sleeping. My BAR man nodded, then grinned. I was in a trance as I sat there, realizing what we had stumbled upon.

I threw one grenade and then the other, following these with six more. Everything happened at once. The confusion and noise were terrific. Above the sound of our firing could be heard Japs screaming. For better than a minute the shooting was all done by us. We were only seven. But the enemy was bunched up and disorganized. Suddenly a heavy machine gun opened fire on us. I don't know where the first burst hit, but the second hit the bank only a few feet below us. The gun was located only 30 yards away and silenced immediately by grenades, BAR and M-1s. At this time one of my men was hit and began sobbing. But the sound stopped as he pulled himself back over the bank. There were a few more scattered 25 caliber rifle shots. Then they fired no more. We finished off any wounded and riddled the huts."

The raid earned Milt a Bronze Star. Thereafter, he sneaked near unsuspecting enemy soldiers on numerous occasions. Once he even penned Peggie a letter within sight of the enemy. "For the past hour I have been watching about 10 Nips take their morning swim," he wrote. "They are about 300 or 400 yards down the stream. The stream is quite large and I have seen many ducks go by. Boy would I like to go hunting." The note ends with a promise: "I will let you know how the whole thing turns out." An update is appended as a postscript. "We've been scouting 'em out for three days," Milt noted. "I've got reinforcements coming and we'll hit them at daybreak… I got within 15 yards of three Nips cutting wood. They were unarmed, but I let them alone as we want to get the whole works. I later crawled to within 10 yards of their garrison. I saw five or six and heard about 20 more jabbering. I've got my plans all laid."

In a turn that made things easier on Peggie, Milt wasn't able to send the letter off until later, when he could include the outcome. "Your hubby is as tired as he has ever been in his life," he explained. "We lay around the Nips for 4 days, finding out all we could about them, and then we hit 'em. Knocked them for a loop. We had no casualties. Just an hour ago the General pinned a medal on me—rather a rushed affair." Nodding to his peril, he added that he enclosed "a little note I wrote to you when way out in the jungle. Save it because it is quite a souvenir, mainly because I am in shape to send it."

The patrol had killed 23 Japanese troops, some at close range, just as they were preparing a surprise offensive. "It was a suicide attack," he noted. "I found their order from their regimental commander. I saw it translated. It directed that every man in the entire group must die to abolish the disgrace incurred when this group had 14 men killed and then retreated when many were too sick to fight."

In fact, the Japanese commander who wrote the order "did not want the men to disgrace themselves further, so he committed suicide to bolster their morale." That staggered Milt. "I held these documents in my hands. I took them from the dead officer's body," he wrote. "When I came overseas I didn't believe such things could happen. I saw one Jap blow his stomach out with a hand grenade only 10 yards from me." These experiences affected the way he and his men fought. "We hit the Japs suddenly. When another officer saw me coming he pulled a blanket he had wrapped around him over his head and just lay quivering," he noted. "I didn't dare take him prisoner as I did not know but what he might have a grenade or knife; so I raked him with my tommy gun."

The operation was a huge success. "We captured machine guns, mortars, automatic rifles, carbines, pistols, quantities of food, ammunition and clothing. The radios will be the most valuable items," he related. "There is always one bad thing about such a patrol. When you come back, a report of the whole affair must be made out in detail. That takes a lot of writing." Once higher-ups reviewed what had transpired they awarded Milt the most prestigious honor he would receive. "The President of the United States takes pleasure in presenting the Silver Star to First Lieutenant Milton C. Shedd for conspicuous gallantry and intrepidity in action..." the citation stated.

"Much valuable information was obtained. His intrepid leadership and selfless devotion to duty, without regard for his own safety, were in keeping with the highest traditions of military service and reflect great credit upon himself, his unit, and the United States Army."

As a reward, Milt was temporarily pulled from his regular duties and tasked with transporting 7 Japanese POWs to Australia, where he would be permitted a short leave. "It will be a business trip," he wrote. "There is nothing especially exciting about my going except I'll see a bit of civilization." That proved a better reward than anticipated. "For the first time in months I looked upon civilians," he wrote from Townsville, Australia. "It was quite a sight seeing family life and routines: father on his way to work, the kids playing in the streets, mother doing her shopping." He enjoyed malted milks, a brief conversation with the first woman he'd spoken to in months, and ice cream. "For a man straight from the front this land is a paradise," he wrote. "In talking to troops stationed here for 18 months, I find that they are all bored, many of them wishing they were up front. The boys here don't realize how well off they are."

When he next wrote home he praised the Red Cross for making officers on leave so comfortable. "I had a wonderful change," he remarked, but "I do not feel right in staying away any longer." Among other things, the vacation from war caused him to reflect on how long some men serving beside him had gone without one. "I recognize the value of my experienced men, but three years overseas is too long for any man," he wrote. "I'd hate to go without them, but I wish they did not have to fight again."

He worried for them. And perhaps for himself. "A man's luck only lasts so long," he wrote. "Or shall we say, the law of chance operates on a mathematical basis: in time percentages and ratios balance as they should." Milt bragged in a late December letter to his father about a saber that he had acquired to hang in the den that he and Peggie were planning, only to add, "I see no hope of my getting home for at least another year or a year-and-a-half at the earliest, unless I am shot up." It wasn't that the Allied war effort was going badly. U.S. Forces were scoring victories across the Pacific, even landing on Leyte in the Philippines. But General MacArthur intended to liberate the whole Philippine archipelago, a plan that other generals thought needless and likely to incur heavy casualties.

On Bougainville, the men were under orders to practice climbing up and down cargo nets, a portent of an amphibious assault to come. Many hated the thought of departing. "Tents had been dressed out with awnings, hammocks had been strung up, and volleyball courts improved with lights," Shoptaugh wrote. "Men made pets of birds. There was body surfing in the bay with mattress covers. Fishing competitions had been common." Starting on January 8, 1945, they left it all behind, braving seas with swells so steep that some feared their transports would capsize. In fact, all arrived in the Philippines without incident, finding a landscape that was "still hot, but not so horribly covered with jungle; much land was cultivated in sugar cane, palm trees, rice, cane and bamboo fields, and some varieties of potatoes. Small hills were the most common military feature." The fighting involved "patrolling and skirmishes with the Japanese units that held out until the last minute and then fled, only to turn up entrenched in another position." The Japanese had neither food supplies nor air support nor heavy artillery, "but their rifles were still accurate," Shoptaugh wrote, "their machine guns still plentifully supplied with ammunition, and their tenacity was only slightly diminished. There were plenty of chances to get killed in a fight that did little to bring the end of the war closer."

Milt shared that assessment. "Our regiment has killed a hell of a lot of Nips," he wrote. "There has been no knock-down drag out fighting… we are doing nothing more than mopping up. These islands may be declared secure but there are still thousands of Nips roaming."

For the rest of the war his correspondence was blunt and gloomy, in part because many of the most dangerous engagements yielded little of strategic importance. When he next wrote–the letter is dated February 28, 1945—he noted "excitement" a thousand yards or so from his position, a desire "to tell you I'm alive and well," and a promise that "by the time you get this, things will have quieted down." He added, "lately I've been dreaming of you every night… but two or three times my midnight reveries have been shattered by the splatter and crackle of rifle and machine gun fire." He closed the note, "See you in a couple of years." On March 7, he penned another letter from harm's way, wishing Peggie "happy anniversary" before writing, "It is raining, but I am in a fox hole covered by a poncho so I'm keeping dry." A battle was before him: "Our boys just took a little knoll from the Nips. Watched the whole show through my scope," he wrote. "I could see them only 10 yards in front of our men. Mortar fire pinned the Nips in their holes and riflemen moved in fast and shot them from close range before they could gather their wits."

He did little patrol work but a lot of fighting. Once, while setting up an observation post, he and his men came under attack. "25 of us held that hill from an equal if not greater number. They threw grenades from less than 10 yards," he wrote. "It was spooky to say the least. None of our men was hurt really bad, but about one-third of our gang was hit with grenade fragment, though not bad enough to collect a Purple Heart."

He called his own wound "only a scratch."

"There is a lot of firing," he wrote a couple days later, adding that every night the enemy rushed their posts on suicide missions. "This keeps us quite jittery," he admitted, "however, nothing will ever affect me as adversely as did that wild bunch of Nips that hit us a few nights ago." The attacks elicited bellicose humor. "I'm getting as I don't like Japs, at least not those with guns," he wrote. "I have a 50 caliber machine gun I use for sniping. It is very effective to about 1500 yards. With my scope I can see them where they think they're safe. But I sure surprise 'em!"

Other times he apologized to Peggie for the effect combat had on their correspondence. "Although you are constantly in my thoughts, I've not felt like writing love letters," he explained. "This outfit has not seen such fighting since Guadalcanal. While far from the most forward elements we have it rough in every respect."

He didn't write again until March 26, 1945. The fighting on Leyte had died down. Most men awaited orders that would determine their next assignment. But Milt's heightened awareness of his mortality didn't prevent him from courting danger, at least not if it got him out on the ocean. "I again went joy riding with the PT boats," he wrote. "We got 5 Nip barges and nearly didn't make it home. We came wedged on a reef only 500 yards off shore from enemy positions. The Nips put better than a hundred holes in our boat wounding several of our men."

They were rescued by another PT boat that braved Japanese fire to successfully pull them off the reef. "I've concluded that I get shot at enough without asking for it unnecessarily," he wrote, "so I doubt if I'll go on any more joy rides with those people."

Only then did he reveal that he was writing the letter from the hospital. A severe cut on his knee was infected and required penicillin shots every four hours. On April 2, 1945, he apologized for how difficult it was to write home, expressed his devotion to Peggie, and added a postscript in small print: "The doctors tell me I have Dengue Fever," he revealed, "and must stay in the hospital."

The disease likely enhanced his safety. In late March and early April, General MacArthur pressed forth with his plan to liberate the Philippine islands, landing forces on Negros, Bohol, and Cebu. More than 1400 died on Negros alone. Landing on Cebu, U.S. forces discovered that the beach was booby trapped. One corporal described men running into a "solid field of mines" and being shredded by "a murderous hail of exploding shrapnel." It was the opposite of sneaking through the jungle on patrols. Men were disemboweled, torn in two, and froze in place even under fire for fear of stepping on land mines. Having finally made it ashore, the surviving men found Cebu City abandoned and proceeded to fight into the hills, where a Japanese commander had dug into hill tops and caves. Casualties were so heavy that help was needed. The 164th headed to Cebu to fight.

Finally out of the hospital and recovered, Milt joined them there on April 22, 1945. He told Peggie, "we have just completed another rat race. The Nips threw everything but the kitchen sink at us, but the American Doughboy can't be beat. Although his buddies go down on all sides he pushes on." Fighting was fierce. "The Nips held all the high ground... and spent months organizing defenses," he wrote. "All hill masses were latticed with an elaborate trench system and pocked with deep caves running 60 to 100 feet into solid rock... Generators provided lighting. Defeat came upon the Nips with such suddenness he was forced to evacuate his positions without destroying them."

Warned of booby traps and snipers, Milt was sent on the first patrol into an area the Japanese had abandoned the prior night. It was the last he would undertake. Like many other experienced officers, he was reassigned to headquarters, where knowledgeable men were needed. Despite having so recently resolved to keep out of harm's way, he was soon plotting how to get back in the fight. "I do not like staff work and want to get back into a line company even if it's only as a platoon leader," he wrote. "I don't like sitting on my fanny while the rest of the boys do all the dirty work."

Fate had other ideas. On April 25, as the 164th made an amphibious landing at the southern tip of Negros, Milt wrote, "I'm very much in the dumps as I've just been sent to the hospital." What he took to be everyday dysentery was diagnosed as amoebic dysentery, "which makes me feel like a shirker." During his sick leave, he encountered victims of Japanese atrocities: Philippine children who had been shot or bayonetted, female prisoners who had been raped and abused. "What they had to say was not complimentary to the Sons of Nippon," he wrote. "I can't understand what prompts a human to cause such needless suffering." If he continued to meet victims of the Japanese army's cruelty, he went on to worry, "I may lose my apathetic feeling in killing Nips and learn to enjoy it."

By May 12, 1945, he was back in combat on Negros, where some assaults were so dangerous that the men assigned to make them talked openly of certain death. "I came straight from the hospital into the hills. I am temporarily back in a line company—my old outfit, E Company," Milt explained. "Although I am only a platoon leader I am happy. We are receiving captains from the states, which sets us all back. The Nips are all around dug into the ridges, living in caves carved in solid rock ledges. We are driving them farther and farther back into the mountains, but it is a slow job… and it takes several hours to evacuate our wounded by native carriers over abysmal trails."

Life on the line meant shells whistling overhead, the crackle of gunfire nearby, and snipers taking pot shots. "Yesterday evening I returned from a long range patrol up the stream bottom for several thousand yards and then up to the top of the ridge," he wrote on May 21. "The object was to come up behind the enemy who were facing one of our companies on the steep razor back. It was some climb — straight up. We bivouacked only 200 yards from the top and my evening security patrol reported Nips just above us." They were gone the next morning. But the knoll they had occupied on the ridge "was an ideal spot for defense, so the company took it over. Last night, the Nips attacked them after I came back down."

Around the same time Milt was promoted. "I am now a company commander," he wrote. He got the news in the hills of Negros, after the fighting had ceased there, while feasting on rations of canned bacon, raisin bread and butter. He and his men were still awaiting orders to withdraw. On June 8, he reported that they had finally descended to the outskirts of a quiet town near the ocean, where the men had three hot meals a day and cots. "The detailed paperwork and little odds and ends that go with garrison type life are quite obnoxious," he complained. "I think I'm a better than average company commander in combat, but I have much to learn in regards of other matters."

As June wore on, he fought enemy holdouts and sent one letter describing the particular strategy at work. "The Japanese are good at organizing and defending prominent terrain features. They are tireless in their effort to dig and build sturdy positions. Their camouflage is a work of art," he wrote. "Because the jungle is so thick and the ridge sides so steep we usually have one avenue of approach—straight up the trail that runs along the ridge tops. The orthodox manner of attacking is to scout up the trail, hoping to see or hear them first, kill a few Nips, and when you have located his positions, pull back a couple hundred yards when things get too hot. Then blow them to pieces with mortar and artillery fire, moving in again quickly before they can reorganize themselves." Casualties abounded. "It's God Damn Dangerous and my hat's off to our scouts that lead the way," Milt wrote. "We can't hope to kill all the Nips. Our objective is to disorganize and scatter them into the hills where they have no supplies."

In July, fighting waned. Milt began getting the company records in order, but so hated paperwork that the task put him in a nasty mood for hours each day. He was finally done by month's end, when the 164th was back on Cebu, once again leading what Milt described as "the garrison type life." He never described the particulars of their training regimen. But everyone was looking ahead to the possibility of invading the Japanese islands.

The Army planned two phases: "The first, an invasion of the southern island of Kyushu, using a task force even larger than employed at the D-Day landings," Shoptaugh wrote. "A study by the Joint Chiefs projected 1.2 million total casualties, with some 300,000 killed." U.S. troops hadn't seen those figures, but knew firsthand that "in defiance of all military logic, the Japanese were willing to die in defense of meaningless ground." What would they do to defend their homeland?

The world would never know.

"News just received of our atomic bombing is quite startling," Milt wrote. "Honey, I'm glad we were the ones to have first perfected their use as this will bring me home sooner, but I am sorry to hear that methods of killing have been advanced to this point. If what I have heard is true, the human race has embarked into a new and perhaps terrible era. Someday, we may be wishing for the days when men fought with clubs."

His next letter was dated August 11: "We are anxiously awaiting you people back home to make up your minds as to whether or not we should accept Japan's surrender terms," he wrote. "Everybody over here says let's call it off. I understand you all think we should kick the emperor out. Perhaps if we hit them with a few more atomic bombs they will surrender unconditionally."

He later described how news of Japan's reaction to Hiroshima reached troops, and how he and his buddies reacted:

"Six of us officers were playing poker. The night was very still and dark as it was about 2100. Suddenly in the distance, perhaps a mile away near regimental headquarters, a hubbub arose. I remarked that there must be a Filipino girl in the area. The sound of voices rolled in on us like the incoming tide. Before long the night was filled with loud hurrahs. Men began screaming. The bottom of my stomach dropped out. Only one thing could affect and disturb combat veterans to such outbursts. Japan had officially thrown in the towel provided we would concede her the point that she be allowed to keep her emperor. Perhaps that will be the best thing for us...

In the meantime we are continuing on with our training as though nothing had happened. For a few hours the men were highly excitable, but in time they quieted down. Next morning at reveille I had a little talk with them explaining just what lay ahead regardless of what happened. It is very gratifying to see their reaction. Instead of behaving in an undisciplined manner they really snap to attention. Morale is sky higher than it's ever been before… If we do decide to take the terms Japan has offered us I don't think I'll be home this year anyway. The important thing is, that I will be coming home alive and in one piece. Someday I'll tell you how many times I almost was rendered asunder."

And on August 15, 1945, he wrote,

"The War is over. I was in bed half asleep on 7 December '41. I could not fully believe we were at war. This morning, after an 8-hour night march, I was in bed and half asleep and heard officially the war was over and could not believe that. But it's true.

We are still continuing with our grinding training schedule but that won't go on forever. I don't see how I'll possibly be home before next spring.

The big job of occupation still lies ahead.

My 62 points should be good for something. I'll take no leave now— when I go home, it's to stay. I love the picture you sent me of your luscious body leaning against a pine at Arrowhead. Oh boy, when I get home!!!

And listen honey, I'm coming home alive and in one big solid piece. Time will drag but my future is assured, so I'm just riding it out without worrying. Promotions may be frozen and I'll come home a 1st lieutenant but I don't care—

I'M COMING HOME!!!"

Six

Letters from the Pacific

World War II was hard on marriages. Beyond its widows, the conflict put hundreds of thousands of couples through more stress than their unions could bear. Deployments prompted many to wed before they were ready; combat changed husbands, who sometimes found girlfriends or fathered children while overseas; wives sometimes sent letters to the front telling stupefied infantrymen, "I don't love you anymore–I won't be waiting when you get home." Statistics tell the story. In 1940 there were 264,000 divorces. The number jumped to 485,000 divorces in 1945 and 610,000 divorces in 1946, a number that wouldn't be equaled for two decades.

But Milt's marriage made it. During two years of fighting that changed him as a person his love for Peggie never wavered. "The boys catch me now and then with a big grin," he once wrote her. "You are the cause, Sweetheart. When I think of what we shall do when I am home, confusion reigns—but there is no confusion concerning my love. It's so simple, it's wonderful! It makes me happy to be so sure. I don't just plain love you; I love you passionately." And she loved him back.

The couple owed their enduring bond largely to correspondence. Husband and wife were so adept at expressing themselves on the page that they learned as much about one another during the war as they had prior to it. Peggie wrote every day. Her letters invariably gave her beloved succor and solace. Milt wrote as often as he could in the most trying times, even as he was sometimes forced to shut out everything, save his surroundings, to survive. The archive of his letters is the best insight into how these newlyweds approached a relationship both treated as precious and permanent.

For Peggie, this meant days or even weeks without news, often because Milt was in danger behind enemy lines. When the mailbox was empty, her religious faith helped her to avoid incessant worry over the possibility that devastating news was on the way. Opening an envelope addressed in Milt's hand was exciting and fraught. Would it be a description of a battle? A complaint about army bureaucracy? A request to develop film? A love letter? A serious reflection on their relationship?

The difficulties of their epistolary marriage are best captured in letters that began on January 1, 1945, just after Milt returned from leave in Australia. "How would you like to throw away your settling down ideas after the war for a few years, and you and I plunge right into a mad adventure?" he wrote. "Why could we not work our way around the world?" What followed was an outpouring, as if hopes and urges bottled up too long burst onto the page. But Milt's excitement was tempered with anxiety about how Peggie might respond. "If we waited until we amassed a fortune we could never make such a trip, because we will probably never amass a fortune," he argued, insistent in one sentence, tentative in the next. "I don't have this 'want to wander' feeling all the time," he hedged. "Sometimes I feel I would like to settle down and live a conventional life. At times the rut appeals to me," he claimed. "Then again, I know that I will be uneasy sitting home living a peaceful and quiet life while still so young."

Then he hit the spacebar twice on his typewriter and changed his tone. "Notice I am telling you my uncontrolled thoughts. I am thinking about what I want to do, not what we want to do," he wrote. "I am alone here, and naturally I think in 'alone' terms. When we are together again you will have a big influence on my thinking, and we may decide that our wild dreams are just wild dreams."

Noting that "what you write will influence my attitudes," he sought a forthright reply. "I have told you my selfish thoughts. If you disagree… come right out and say so. If you want babies right away and a quiet, peaceful home, sum up your fortitude and tell me. Perhaps you don't have that adventurous spirit that I have deep down inside," he wrote. "If not, then I must quench that little flame before it grows big. Now is the time to talk."

Said a handwritten postscript,

> *"I had a rather exciting day and naturally my impulses of the moment have influenced this, so if you want a quiet life to start off and are afraid I'll be hard to tame, have no fears: you have a knack of making me happy in every way and situation. Naturally, I will want to finish college before starting any wild Seven Seas journey. P.S. We could make millions writing of the adventures we might have together."*

Such was the pressure born by the era's marriages: a young man's wanderlust stoked by war; an idea building in his imagination and shared not in its infancy, as in domestic life, but as a fully-formed proposal to alter life plans. Then a week or two passes as the letter is delivered; another week, or two, or even three is spent awaiting a reply. Even at a remove of more than 70 years, it is easy to feel for young Peggie receiving that letter; and for Milt as he awaited her response. Both were intelligent, stubborn people with strong opinions and senses of self. Milt could be brash, obstinate, and condescending. His personality was a confounding mix of empathy, emotional intelligence, and a blunt style of communicating that could be needlessly hard on its recipient. Peggie forgave his faults, for he was lovable, mindful of her happiness, and moral: she had absolute confidence in his honesty, fidelity, and forthrightness. While he could be condescending, she never doubted his respect for her intellect. She had the confidence to hold her own when he became overbearing; the smarts to check his ego; and the maturity to influence his uncontrolled thoughts.

For all that, only a mutual willingness to work hard at communicating got them through. And that had always been true. In college, they had gone back and forth about religion, politics, and philosophy, Milt barreling ahead with frank pronouncements about why he was right; Peggie less needful of winning for its own sake but determined to represent her convictions. Once they argued for hours beneath a street light. "I started a wild discussion that became very involved," Milt confessed in a war letter. "I wanted to know you and become very close to you. I saw in you all I could ever expect of any girl— I did not want to lose you. I was afraid we would bust up if we kept on as we had been doing."

Their shorter arguments often ended with Milt feeling as if he hadn't articulated himself well enough. Surely if he could just find the proper words, she would see things as he did! He would sit up late writing out arguments in notebooks meant for academic assignments. Sometimes the exercise helped him to better express his views, but as often, proceeding without Peggie there to temper his thoughts resulted in manifestos more uncontrolled than what they were meant to clarify.

By the time Milt shipped out he was better at reining in his impulse to argue every point; he would occasionally acknowledge flaws in his thinking, though he sometimes lectured Peggie even while admitting error. Once Peggie gave him advice on writing, adding, "Lover, please don't think I am trying to be a teacher." He replied, "But you are my teacher. Why disclaim your title? You sounded apologetic for helping me. I don't like that. You are better versed in the subject."

He pledged to love her for improving him.

"I am a conceited fellow and know that I have talent in certain lines, but you are superior to me in many ways. If you weren't I'd never have fallen in love with you," he wrote. "Frankly, I like and need you to deflate my ego occasionally. You are much more interesting and I appreciate you more when you do this."

And her influence did change him.

At UCLA, one recurring argument that they had concerned the 1939 book *Language in Thought and Action*. Acknowledging that he ran its subject, semantics, into the ground, frustrating Peggie so much that it became "strictly dynamite," he promised to correspond more circumspectly. Whether writing or fighting, he posited, a person ought to be deliberate, reflective, and concentrate on improving oneself. "It applies equally to thinking," he declared. "But do people spend time thinking about thinking? Obviously not!" He described the discipline:

> "Instead of standing off away from a problem and examining it under the light of conventional dogmatism and prejudice, it involves tearing into the issue tooth and claw, viewing the thing under every possible light... it involves the use of factual evidence that can be verified in the external world. It eliminates wishful thinking and self-hypnotism."

But Peggie could not forget the role Milt's attitude toward thinking had played in their courtship, when she wanted to revel in love and he never went long without probing its qualities. "I wish that you could understand me when I say that you can do too much 'thinking about thinking,'" she warned. "Some things are of too little importance to wear yourself ragged on, and others (along emotional lines in particular) have a great part of their beauty destroyed by exposure to cold hard facts. I maintain that the object of life is to be happy, and if you tear certain things all down they become wearisome and boring, and we lose interest in them."

"How well I understand this," Milt replied. "I use Semantics as a guide for enjoying life just as you use your knowledge of art to enjoy a painting. When you studied art, you did a lot of detailed thinking. Now you enjoy it without that process. In Semantics, you must first experience a period of mental gymnastics; then you will acquire its use naturally. Through experience you habitually think efficiently, so there is generally no need to 'tear things apart' to keep out of trouble. But when the need arises you can see to the bottom of things."

This approach to thinking is evident in many of Milt's letters. In one, he conversed with Peggie about Japan's future even as he fought the country. After an Allied victory, he wondered, how would the Japanese people rejoin the world? "Reasoning will again be on abstract levels and the whole thing will end up being an issue of ideals," he predicted. "Your very letter," he told his wife, "your use of words like 'Heathen,' 'Christianity,' and 'Imperialism,' show that you're thinking of the problem in terms of conventional abstractions."

"I have never seen a thing called Democracy," he wrote. "I have seen a government collecting garbage, taxes, and statistics. I have seen it building roads. But I've never seen this thing called Democracy." As he saw it, "we have taken a million and one things, bundled them all up neatly, and called the whole mess Democracy... we will try to settle the question, both ourselves and the Nips, by arguing about these high order abstractions."

He urged a contrary approach.

"Sooner or later people will get down to explaining the word in terms of bread and butter, houses, and being happy. The Nips will do the same. I have read their mail. The Nip is homesick just as we are. It appears possible, then, that our two systems have something in common... We are all interested in eating, making love, and having friends. I doubt very much if the Nip is interested in Democratic Christianity because he has never had any connection with it except to die because of it."

His dismissal of Democratic Christianity hinted at a larger disagreement with Peggie: she had faith; he preferred empiricism. "I can just see you with your back to the wall stamping your foot and defending your belief in religion for all you are worth," he wrote. "Honey, I'll never interfere in what you want." Thereafter is a glimpse at Milt's ego made palatable by a pinch of self-awareness. "I like discussing the subject with you very much, but I rather imagine you will run away from any such discussions, as I'll probably tear your arguments to pieces, at least to my way of thinking," he wrote. "But in your mind you will probably be laughing at me, and running because you think it foolish to become involved in futile argument with a heathen."

True to his word, religious differences never came between Milt and Peggie. For all his stubbornness and need to see to the bottom of things, he understood that they were beginning a family, not drafting a joint statement on metaphysics, epistemology, or theology. They would become business partners too: Peggie played an active role supporting virtually every aspect of Milt's career. Their correspondence provided a foundation for this partnership. She would express interest in the minutiae of his military duties. He would share his aspirations, his frustrations with higher-ups in the ranks, various problems that he was puzzling out, and explanations of certain actions he took.

Once, he wrote about a man under his command who "thought his was a perfect marriage, but out of a clear sky his wife asked for a divorce… although he has been pleading for more information, she has not written since." Milt wrote to the subordinate's estranged wife, then solicited Peggie's thoughts on the letter:

Dear Mrs. _____

Your husband is a member of my company and since a soldier overseas has no one other than his Company Commander from whom he may seek advice he has come to me. Please don't feel that I am butting into your affairs. Because the lives of men in combat are trying beyond the limits of imagination without being further complicated by the worries of domestic life, I feel it is my obligation to my men to make them as comfortable mentally and physically as I can. So please consider me a friend who is trying to do his duty…

Jerry is still very much in love with you and believes that you still love him. He thinks it not an impossibility that some other difficulty has caused you to seek a divorce. He is convinced that two people in love and determined to enjoy life in the future can overcome any problem by working together, provided all facts and circumstances are made known. Jerry likewise understands that the difficulty may be as you say—that you no longer love him, and if this is truly the case he realizes a divorce would be the best thing. The point is, he has lived with you, loved you, and does not understand this 'bolt out of the blue.' You are not being fair in giving so little information. After all, he has a very large decision to make.

I am a married man myself. My wife and I are both 22. I've had some fair opportunities to view the mental functioning of young women. What they most lack is courage, intestinal fortitude. They are afraid of facts. They hesitate to speak with frankness for fear of the resulting effect on people— i.e. their husbands, boyfriends or fiancés in particular. They are often times quite inconsiderate of others and are not as capable as they might be in seeing and understanding the other person's attitudes or point of view. Of course I am speaking in general terms and this may or may not apply to you; but it seems to me that you have not been showing your husband the consideration he deserves.

You owe Jerry a two-fold obligation. He is your husband and he is a fighting man doing a tough, dirty job a long way from home. You must put time and effort into your letters to clear the matter up. Marriage is a corporation of two people. Rather than deciding what's to be done, you should let him know all the facts and then work out the solution together.

These lines capture so much about Milt: the immaturity of a 22-year-old who sees only cowardice and no wisdom in holding one's tongue; the commitment to forthrightness and cooperation in marriage; and a blunt, unsparing approach that Milt saw as pragmatic, even as his effectiveness was as likely hindered as heightened. If Peggie took any umbrage at the letter's sexism, her reaction was tempered by the fact that in seeking her advice he was implicitly valuing her judgment.

As Milt's time in combat wore on, the optimism of his early letters, replete with frequent descriptions of his adventures, gave way to that period of more intense fighting and less regular correspondence. "My letters are becoming fewer… My life I lived with you is so much in contrast to what it is here," he explained. "The tension is of such a nature that it is difficult to mix or dwell upon the old. There are times when I just cannot sit down and write about home, my wife, etc., so strong is my feeling that all this must be put aside until the mess has been straightened out." He pleaded for patience: "If my letters are too far apart and don't contain the things we both want to say… if there is no mail for my honey today, or if what does arrive isn't as expressive as it might be, I want her to know that Milt is completely and madly in love with every little bit of her." He sounded more reflective, self-aware, and mature. "Tonight I simply had to tell you how beholden I am to you, my sweet, for giving this pining, far away boy so much," said one note. "You stand for everything 'bright and gay' in my life. I know that my letters do not and cannot express my appreciation for all that our marriage means."

He thanked Peggie for the part she played in his transformation. Before, he confessed, he had tried to prove himself by being dominating, quick-witted, and pretentious. He was too inconsiderate in his dealing with others. Peggie set him straight. "You stepped into the picture as an example of unpretentiousness and simplicity of manner," he wrote. "You helped me see that the next man enjoys his theories and convictions as much as I do mine. I have noticed a difference. My relationship with other men is less strained. My old ego doesn't mean so much to me since I've learned to control its growling."

With Japan's surrender, his letters changed a final time. They grew wistful, as when he sat beneath the stars on a barracks bag, watching his men sip beer and sing songs. "Here and there are a very few men that I classify as duds," he wrote. "Most are smiling, reliable, cooperative, and intelligent, with that all-important abstract quality known as courage. Yes Sweetheart," he confessed, "I'll miss the past, days of hard living, danger, strain, excitement, and comradeship. But I'm thankful they are past. I'm satisfied that we've earned the right to return home and live the lives we desire."

That was the other change. For the first time in months, Milt permitted himself to plan beyond the war. And he surprised Peggie by airing another course they had never discussed. "If the army allows officers to close their theater and take their wives overseas, providing they sign up for three years, such a proposition might be worth looking into," he wrote. "How would you react to three more years army life providing we could go to Europe, where I could finish college?" He added, "When the three years were up we could settle down and start our family… Of course, such a thing might be out of the question, but at least it's worth thinking about. Please write me your reaction… I'll do nothing before I find out complete information and discuss with you."

Planning his homecoming was more straightforward. "Would you think it silly if I told you that I would like to spend our first couple of nights when I come home at the Biltmore Hotel in the Bridal Suite where we so happily began our married life?" he asked. "We have been apart so long that we'll feel like we are being married all over, and for such a momentous occasion I don't think we should worry too much about expense." He didn't want any delay.

"Honey, for the first few days of my return, I don't want to be with anybody but my DEAR SWEET WIFE, so I'd like to take a short run-away trip," he wrote from Japan at the beginning of the occupation. "I will not be interested in driving hundreds of miles to go hunting and fishing," he added, marking the last time in their lives that he wouldn't want to fish on vacation. "I will want to go to a nice, quiet place where we can live together, alone, enjoying the luxuries of civilization. I think great of my family, but now, I belong to you and you belong to me and by that token we belong together, first, last and most of the time. I've fought for you all the time I've been gone," he declared, "and I'll fight for you when I come home, only then we'll lick the world fighting side by side."

Seven

THE BABY BOOM

Milt and Peggie chose Palm Springs, California, for that "quick runaway trip" together. Alone at the desert resort they reveled in one another's company. He was lean, tanned, and handsome, muscles still hard from soldiering. Gorgeous in her bathing suit, she beckoned him into the swimming pool one day, perhaps sensing that he needed more excitement amid all their relaxation.

"Do you want to race?" she challenged.

Milt grinned. He was well rested, as fit as he had ever been in his life, and not so far removed from the South Seas riptides he had bested while training to swim in combat. He agreed to race, as she knew that he would. And then he was stunned, and she grinning, for she touched the wall first. He hated losing, but loved having married a woman who could best him. She was triumphant—and so tickled by his surprise in defeat that she laughed telling the story more than 60 years later.

In those first weeks home Milt's happy moments were many: a first glimpse of American soil; Peggie's body in his arms, her lips pressed to his; a handshake from a father beaming with pride at his warrior son; a mother teary-eyed at his safe return; seeing Maria, who no longer needed to pray for Milt on her rosary; and Ruthie, who had given birth to a baby girl, his first niece. Sadness intruded too. Milt's dog, Phantom X, had died shortly before his master's return; and happy reunions with friends would often come around to tragedy. "Did you hear that ____ was killed? His wife has been so strong; tragic the child never knew him." Most survivors felt some guilt.

The intense emotions of homecoming then gave way to a new feeling: ennui. In civilian life, there were neither orders to obey nor superiors to please nor battles to fight. There was no camaraderie, no overwhelming purpose, no epic triumphs, no deep despair. And whereas a surviving North Dakotan could swap the adrenaline of warrior life for something like their prewar existence, with hometowns and landscapes mostly unchanged, the California known to Milt was gone. 3 million people had moved to California, many of them to Los Angeles.

"Lots that sold for $850 during the war jumped to $5,000 by 1946," historian Kevin Starr writes. "Even buyers who had made their down payments had to wait eight or nine months, even a year, as material shortages, compounded by a shortage of carpenters, electricians, plumbers, and other building trade workers, brought development after development to a grinding halt."

With dreams of buying that house with a den, Milt and Peggie had saved diligently throughout the war. Milt had even managed to win enough at poker on the troop transport home to buy a car. But the couple's savings had to carry them through Milt's final year at UCLA, where students were so hard up for housing that some lived in converted streetcars or airplane fuselages. As their second honeymoon in the desert ended, moving in with Peggie's widower mother was their best option.

Milt's return to UCLA was another reminder that he couldn't reclaim his pre-war life. The classrooms, athletic fields, and frat houses were the same. But the students were different. The boys, the lucky ones, had come back. And they were men. Other veterans matriculated through the G.I. Bill. "That first semester, there were fifty," Andrew Hamilton writes in *UCLA On The Move*, an official history. "This trickle swelled into a mighty flood by September 1947, when 6,255 ex-servicemen enrolled, 43 percent of the student body. They were older than previous college generations, more interested in vocationally-oriented courses, and many were married, giving the student body an overall maturity and seriousness of purpose."

Milt personified that change in UCLA's undergraduates. He spent dramatically less time at the frat house and attended fewer parties. No longer content with average grades, he earned straight As—it took far less discipline than running a rifle company, a contrast that kept returning to his thoughts as *UCLA Magazine* ran profiles on students who had died overseas.

Family life added to Milt's new outlook: in his final year of classes, he had a pregnant wife. Telling the news to his father was a happy moment: all Milton Senior's life, family mattered to him most. How glorious that his son would be a dad! And he felt certain that Peggie would make a wonderful mom. The Depression days that Milton Senior had spent unemployed were long gone. Still deep in debt when World War II began, he had worked tirelessly for the duration, his engineering skills in high demand. The long hours wore him down, but he paid back all his creditors, taking pride that he never discharged a debt. He was even able to buy 15 acres of land in the Baldwin Hills, planning to subdivide it among his children so that the whole family could live close to one another. Now he imagined his little grandson coming of age there.

As the due date approached the usual preparations were made: the couple kept the doctor's phone number handy, learned the best route to the hospital, and bought a crib. Peggie went into labor one evening that January. At the hospital, Milt turned her over to the nurses and retired to the waiting room, where he spread out textbooks and notes, for it was exam week.

In the delivery room, alone but for the doctor and nurses, Peggie had contractions, and the umbilical cord wound its way around the baby's neck. "Every time I had pain his heart would stop," she remembered. "It was a scary thing to go through."

The hospital finally apprised Milt—not that he could offer anything beyond moral support. "But we always seemed able to get through the scary things very well together," Peggie recalled. And so it happened on that occasion. After spending all night in labor, Peggie gave birth to their first-born by emergency cesarean section. They named him Steven. The birth took on even greater meaning a few months later, when the family was surprised by an untimely death: Milton Senior suffered a fatal heart attack at 60. His survivors took comfort that he lived to hold his first grandson.

For Milt and Peggie, the challenges of being new parents eased their mourning. As they settled into family life, Gov. Earl Warren gave a speech about the challenges confronting young adults of their generation: a housing shortage, schools packed to suffocation, a dangerous, inadequate highway system. "Living in a society in which too much was happening too soon," says historian Kevin Starr, describing the period, "Californians were forced to line up to rent an apartment, to buy an automobile, to register a child in school, to purchase any number of durable goods in short supply, or to eat in a restaurant."

The San Fernando Valley was one result. House builders developing a 235-square-mile area where the population more than doubled between 1945 and 1950. Amid the boom, stock brokerages quickly moved to create new sales territory, hoping to win over upwardly mobile residents. Several firms were eager to hire a decorated war hero, UCLA graduate and new father. And Milt was eager, in turn, to try his hand as a broker.

He exuded hard-charging enthusiasm, and declined one job offer with a guaranteed salary, reasoning that it would be fairer for all parties if he were paid on performance. At first, that conviction hurt his income. Meeting prospects on behalf of a firm where he worked on commission, he urged a conservative approach: buy a diversified portfolio of safe stocks and hold them. Potential customers who wanted a different approach got unsolicited lectures instead. "He just knew to his core that these people should do what he told them," Peggie remembered. "But they didn't want to hear from some whippersnapper just starting out that their ideas were wrong."

Still, he wasn't satisfied making a commission. He wanted to be scrupulous, to sell them what would pay off in the long run, even when they said that they didn't want it. With fewer commissions coming in as a result, savings that had dwindled by design while Milt finished at UCLA now shrank by necessity. He needed new suits for his sales job, gas to get from the office to his sale territory, and all the odds and ends of child-rearing. Fruitless days of work were discouraging, but he kept at it, tapping friends, following leads, even knocking on doors and cold-calling. He would start early in the morning, arriving at the office before the markets opened. Sometimes he wouldn't return home until seven or eight. As encouragement, Peggie promised to prepare his favorite, homemade ice cream, on days when he hit a modest sales target. "For a long time," she remembered, "he very rarely got any ice cream."

With time, however, new clients were won; some perceived and appreciated Milt's honesty; these happy few referred others. There was no single breakthrough. But one client's decision to give Milt his business squared so perfectly with his father's values that it made its way into Shedd family lore. As the story goes, Milt was still struggling to find customers when he cold-called this fellow with his usual pitch. The prospect, an older man, wasn't interested until he heard Milt's family name. "Listen," he said. "Is your father's name Milton Shedd too? Are you that man's son?" Milt said that he was.

"Your father owed me a lot of money during the Depression," the man said. "He could have declared himself bankrupt, but he paid me back every penny. If you've got half the integrity of your father I'd be honored to give you my business." It felt, to Milt, like his father's moral teachings had been vindicated. Keeping one's word, especially in situations where few other men would have felt compelled to do so, was both a moral good and an investment: if a man didn't sully his character he'd benefit his soul and his reputation in the long run.

Slowly, the Shedd savings account recovered. Milt started to fish more regularly, to pitch in a recreational baseball league, and to play handball— he once beat the national champion in a tournament at the Los Angeles Athletic Club and took noontime losses hard enough to lament his defeats at family dinners.

He flirted with politics too. His interest wasn't unexpected. He had run for student leadership at UCLA and often mused on the responsibility he felt to help shape society. "I'll never be a robed fanatic, but I see so many damn things that need straightening out," he wrote Peggie during the war. "People try to better conditions by running away from the logical solution. They become involved in abstractions rather than putting their nose to the ground to find out what is going on!" To involve himself in problem-solving, Milt co-founded the first Young Republicans chapter in North Hollywood. He then rose in the Los Angeles County Young Republicans, eventually becoming their executive vice-president.

Had he so chosen, he could have become an influential player in state politics, improving civic life with his pragmatism and aversion to mendacity. But L.A. County politics in that era was shaped by a local congressman, Richard Nixon, who had his eye on a Senate seat and had presumably begun dreaming of the White House. Being around Nixon and his associates made Milt uneasy. Although he agreed with their conservatism, he quickly perceived that men in their world were constantly pressured to compromise themselves and often did. Buying votes. Disingenuously telling people what they wanted to hear. Amassing power for its own sake. Milt abhorred such behavior, and was never one to try to stay pure among the sullied—if he saw dishonesty, his impulse was to disassociate from the liar. He quit the GOP.

1949 would be busy enough. The brokerage business was more than a full-time job. He fished as often as he could. A dutiful patriot, he had joined the National Guard, drilling a weekend per month. He and Peggie volunteered as alumni advisors at the fraternity. And most important of all, Carol Shedd was born.

The new baby added to Milt's desire for their own space. Peggie's mother always wanted her son-in-law to help more with yard work and odd jobs. For Milt, who had been evading chores since childhood, placating her was a slog. As a busy young man stretched thin at work and at play, the notion of foregoing a Saturday fishing trip or an hour with his new baby to mow the lawn made moving the best option. Milt and Peggie eventually found an apartment in North Hollywood. The home proved a satisfying symbol of independence to both. No matter that they were poor. They were a young family, happily in love, possessed of what they needed, and confident that they would know material success in time, even if Milt was impatient for a breakthrough. On his worst days, it sustained him to return to the peaceful home Peggie created, to her relentlessly supportive attitude and sage advice.

By spring 1950 they had settled into a happy domestic routine. They seldom argued. "I remember there was a freezer I wanted to buy on time," Peggie said. Neither she nor Milt was inclined to purchase anything on credit. "But I thought that in this case, if I had a freezer, I could buy meat in bulk from the butcher, pay a lower price, and save money," said Peggie, who pressed her husband by projecting out the expected savings. "We usually did things the way that Milt wanted to do them," she explained, "but whenever I felt very strongly about something, I would somehow manage to get my way in the end."

By April, 1951, Peggie was pregnant again. That summer, she was reminded how oppressively hot it could be in North Hollywood, under the San Fernando Valley sun. "I'd be stuck in that hot apartment, no car, unable to run any errands or go anywhere," she said. "Milt would brag sometimes about how many diapers he washed. He never touched any diapers." Their third child, Bill, was born that winter. The period was tough for Peggie. Her husband worked long hours. And she got no respite on weekends. Milt would awake in the pre-dawn hours, climb into the family car, and drive to Santa Monica or San Pedro or Long Beach, where he would fish all day. Often he didn't return until after dark. If the fish were really biting or he had gone far offshore he would be away until Sunday morning.

To rationalize these forays, Milt would think not only of his compulsion to fish, but of the opportunity sportfishing provided to meet and socialize with clients and prospects. It was a self-serving story. "A few times, I got so angry that I'd take my typewriter out after the kids had gone to bed and leave him a long letter of complaint," Peggie said. "He would apologize. It never was a big thing. I never saved any of those letters." Peggie's distaste for the heat nevertheless played a part in the couple's decision to move. Intent on buying in cooler climes, they gravitated toward Orange County. In the 1950s, vast tracts of citrus farms and chaparral were developed into subdivisions with wide, quiet streets. Early in their house hunt, Milt decided a long commute on potholed streets would be worth it if he could live beside the ocean. Peggie wanted to live near enough to schools that her kids could walk there.

Kings Road in Newport Beach met all their conditions. The street sat on a bluff overlooking Newport Harbor. A grammar, middle, and high school were steps away. Milt still obsessed over the potential purchase, researching every detail and pressing Peggie into seemingly endless discussions of variables big and small. But once they decided on a course of action he never looked back. The couple bought a three-bedroom house in 1954. He lived there for the rest of his life. Fetching the newspaper, he could look out at the bay. To save on gas he bought a small car, a Renault, for his long commute. Squeezing into it took a toll on his back, but he liked a long route that permitted him to drive for awhile on Coast Highway, past oil derricks that dotted the Huntington Beach coastline. Leaving before dawn, he arrived at work before the markets opened, played handball at lunch, finished work when the markets closed in New York, and drove home to his kids.

Steve, Bill, and Carol did most of their growing up on Kings Road, completing chores in the yard and homework at the kitchen table. Peggie typically prepared dinner, often cooking what Milt caught. The kids grew up eating halibut, white seabass, tuna, grouper—nearly every fish save for mackerel. Milt would occasionally dig for clams in a nearby marshland. Once, he brought home a spider crab that walked across the driveway. Another time he trapped lobsters so big that he had to borrow a pot from a local seafood restaurant to cook them.

His children were fondest of the times when he harvested abalone. They would watch impatiently as he removed the meat from the shells and cut it into patties. The fun began when he grabbed his special wooden mallet, raised it over his head in an exaggerated motion, and brought it down with gusto, hammering the patties paper thin. Peggie didn't mind doing the breading and frying, and loved eating abalone, but wasn't fond of the fact that Milt's hammering spread bits of shellfish all over the kitchen, which she was always left to clean up.

Steve's first memory of his father is standing in a North Hollywood backyard at age three or four learning to play catch. His earliest memory of Newport Beach, where he moved at 7, is taking a batter's stance while his dad, the former pitcher, taught him to swing. These scenes have a Norman Rockwell quality. But for Milt, introducing his boys to sports wasn't ritual or leisure, nor was it an excuse to spend more time with them. Sports were the way a young man prepared for life.

Milt had felt himself at a disadvantage in childhood when his father would be off working while the dads of his grammar school classmates taught them to throw, catch, and tackle. He struggled to excel at games his peers knew better, and hated losing so much that small setbacks would make him self-conscious and trigger his temper. But he eventually realized, through observation, that mental toughness often mattered most. Even as his technique improved, he worked to steady his nerves and control his emotions on the pitcher's mound. That skill helped to keep him alive in war, where he felt grateful for his hard-won ability to assess his mindset with remove, to quiet self doubt, and to perform under intense pressure.

With sons of his own, he felt a responsibility to prepare them as fully for whatever a nasty, brutish world might bring. Cold War saber-rattling only increased his pessimism about the future. His sons would learn to control their emotions as he had; and if ever they faced a moment that would wipe out all but the fittest, the Shedd boys would make it. "He was imparting tools of survival," Steve remembers. "And we felt that intensity."

As the oldest, Steve experienced his dad's parenting at its most intense. At 5, when Milt thought he was clinging too much to childish things, he invited him out to wash the car, a treat at that age. "He made sure to say I should bring my blankie. And that old blankie didn't have a chance," Steve said. "By the time we were done drying the car it was all used up." The next year, having practiced pushups at his dad's urging, the 6-year-old did fifty in a row to win a YMCA contest.

When a father goes fishing every weekend a boy soon wants to join him, and by age eight Steve was begging to go along. Milt showed his son a buoy a couple hundred yards from shore. "When you can swim out and back," he said, "then you can come." Impatient, Steve practically drowned himself to earn a spot on the boat, only to get severely seasick on the water his first time out. His dad promised it would get better. Several tries later, the eight-year-old knew he would never be a fisherman. He just couldn't take the sea's ups-and-downs.

Thereafter, Milt's time with Steve revolved around sports. He perceived that his son was too sensitive during his earliest outings as a Little League pitcher to opponents jeering from the opposing dugout. When they next went to the park to practice Milt heckled Steve while he threw pitches. "Hey you jerk!" he would shout. "Oh, I knew you'd hear me, rabbit ears! I knew I could make you cry, you big cry baby!" If he brought his son to tears it was just evidence of the need for the exercise. "He wanted to prepare me for battle," Steve reflected. "It was always just me and him at the park when he did that. He'd never humiliate me in front of other people. He just thought that if I had enough practice I could overcome my bad feelings."

The poem "If" was one of Milt's lodestars, and Steve came to know Kipling's words: "If you can meet with Triumph and Disaster and treat those two impostors just the same... you'll be a Man, my son!" Milt trained his eldest to be neither too high in victory nor too low in defeat. "When dad competed, or even when he played cards or invented some game, it was very important to him that he won," Steve recalled, "but with Billy and I, it was only important that we do our best and maintain the right attitude no matter what happened."

In high school, where Steve played baseball and football, Milt never tired of throwing him pitches and even gave the school money to build a weight room where its athletes could prepare. Steve often felt lucky to have his father so involved. Coaches respected him. Steve knew he had a supporter on the sidelines. And Milt was no mere spectator: he would be in the stands with a Super 8 camera filming so that the team could gather afterward at the high school or the Shedd house to learn from key plays. Years later, when Steve found boxes of old family films, he gave them to a friend for transfer onto VHS, thinking there would be vacation footage and family memories. But the overwhelming majority of the reels contained minor variations on the same utilitarian game footage: a center hiking the ball to Steve, who would hand it off or drop back into the pocket to throw a forward pass. For Milt, the film was never about memories. It was for self-improvement.

At times, Milt took the "stop crying and get on with life" attitude to imprudent extremes. That's when Steve felt less lucky. At 15, he was the football team's quarterback, though he was small for his age. He got sacked so hard by a bigger boy that his collar bone snapped. He fainted coming off the field.

"I was in over my head. I didn't even have hair under my arms yet," he said. "I was glad I got hurt." It was such a bad break that he missed four or five days of school. His parents wanted him back as soon as possible but his cast was breaking down.

"I said, 'Dad, I can't go to school.'"

"But he said, 'Bullshit, you're going,' and he brought me into the garage, where the first thing he sees is electrical tape. Now, once you got him going, there's no stopping him, so he kept wrapping the cast very securely. And when he finally ran out of tape he said, 'Okay, that'll do.' A guy who went on patrols during the war, a broken bone wasn't a big deal to him."

Later that morning, during Steve's first period class, his teacher looked at him in horror. "Steven, you're white!" she said. Milt had unwittingly cut off his circulation. "The nurse cut me loose and they sent me to the doctor," Steve recalled. "That was Dad." And the imprudent extreme had yet to come.

"At that point we had five weeks left in the season," Steve said. "Well, my dad went to a family friend who was a doctor and said, 'I want you to sign off on my son.' Today, if you get a compound fracture, you can't do anything for 6 months. But the coach had promised that he would only use me if I was needed on a few passing plays." On game night, Steve took the field.

"I completed passes on successive plays. I looked over at the coach, and he said, 'Run it again.' If I get hit I'm done. But I ran it again. And I got hit. I knew I would re-break it. But Dad wanted me to play. He thought, it's healed, he can throw, he's a big boy. When you've seen friends die in battle, watched the sorts of injuries that he witnessed, I can see why you wouldn't have as much sympathy as a normal person for a broken shoulder."

"For dad," Steve repeated, "sports were a way to hone your ability to compete, test yourself, and learn life lessons without losing your life if you failed. It was necessary for survival, because prior planning prevents poor performance. If you invested time and energy to prepare, you put yourself in a position to succeed." Steve went on to play professional baseball in Italy.

With Carol, fewer opportunities to play sports meant getting somewhat less of her father's time, though she experienced Milt's softer qualities in a way her two brothers didn't. "My first recollection of dad was seeing his strong legs on a ladder he ascended to the loft in a cabin we rented," she recalls. "Being inquisitive, I followed him up, let go before the top, and ended up with a cracked skull." She suffered terrible headaches as a result. "Dad would have me lie flat on my back, take deep breaths, and imagine that I was floating into the clouds," she said. "He would instruct me to think about my toes floating down slowly, then my legs getting heavy and sinking, then my stomach and my arms, until he reached the top of my head; he would continue sitting with me until he relaxed every bone head to toe and I was out like a light."

She remembers Milt's Tarzan yell, accompanied by enthusiastic chest beating, which he let loose to delight her. After dinner, he would sometimes go into Carol's room to play a miniature piano that the family kept there. And she remembers him singing along to the soundtrack from South Pacific.

But Milt was at his most ham-fisted as a parent when called on to empathize with an adolescent girl. When Carol was 11 she was a bit heavy and lacked self-esteem, often walking around all stooped over. Milt's practical inclinations led him astray — without consulting Carol, he ordered a harness for her to wear. The day it arrived in the mail he encouraged her to put it on, explaining that it would correct her posture.

Perhaps it was fortuitous that Steve got too seasick to fish, for Carol loved going out on the water, and the outings afforded many opportunities for happier moments with her father. They would sometimes leave the house together after midnight on a weekday— in a family where even a decaying cast was no reason to miss school, fishing was a special exception. They drove down a Pacific Coast Highway so deserted that Milt coasted through red lights, arriving in Long Beach with plenty of time to spare and shoving off before dawn on a half-day recreational fishing boat where Milt invariably caught more than his share. Carol especially remembers a 250-pound black seabass that he caught. "All we had was a yellow Renault to take our monster fish home," she said. "So where else could we put it but the trunk in the front of the car? This was rush hour. The head and tail were visibly sticking out. We were lucky we weren't stopped by the police."

Even as a little girl, she was conscious of how seriously her father took fishing. "On my tenth birthday, dad and I caught the boat at midnight and arrived at Catalina Island early in the morning, where Dad spotted a school of white seabass boiling around the boat," she remembers. "Soon I was hooked up to one. I yelled 'color' and the deckhand appeared with the gaff. Then, I couldn't believe it: a giant black seabass was suddenly going after my white seabass, which took off beneath the boat and wrapped the line around the propeller. That giant black seabass vanished. 'But what about my white seabass?' I cried. Dad said, 'No problem, I'll jump off the back and untangle the line.' That was Dad. Who else would have thought to take fins and a diving mask on a recreational fishing boat? Dad was always prepared for anything."

Milt's youngest son, Bill, benefitted from his father's efforts to improve his parenting. Whereas Steve was heckled to teach him the importance of good feelings, Bill remembers an afternoon before he was a teenager when his father took him to a high school football game. They climbed up into the bleachers and Milt told his son, "Look out there. Who do you think is the most confident boy? Who is the most popular girl?" Bill pointed down at the quarterback of the football team and the most beautiful of the cheerleaders. "Do you know what those two are thinking right now?" Milt asked. "That quarterback is thinking, 'Oh man, I don't know if I'm good enough to be here. I'm nervous that I'm going to make a mistake and coach is going to pull me out.' And do you know what that cheerleader is thinking? 'I'm not as pretty as the other girls, none of the boys like me, everyone is talking behind my back.'"

As ever, Milt made the lesson explicit. "I know it's hard to believe, Billy," he said, "but everyone in high school gets very self-conscious. I'm telling you now, so that when you get there and it happens to you, it isn't nearly as bad. Remember, everyone around you is thinking the same thing—and no one is thinking about you." Bill did remember years later, when he was quarterback of the Newport Harbor High football team and dating a cheerleader. The bygone talk worked exactly as intended, giving him perspective in adolescence relative to his peers.

Bill would spend more time with Milt than either of his siblings: like Steve, he was an athlete with early memories of learning to throw, catch, and swing. And like Carol, he loved to fish and spent countless hours on the ocean with his dad. As well, there were times when he missed his dad, along with his siblings, because Milt was off conducting business or fishing on his own. Those days and nights away at sea were a reality that Peggie lived with throughout their marriage. "When you have a passion like that you can't help but embrace it," she said, "which I always knew and tried my best to understand." Early on, when Milt could have found new clients at a golf club or church or fraternal organization, Peggie couldn't know that her indulgence of her husband's fishing trips would prove as important to his career as to the health of their marriage. But as it turned out, the great rationalization of Milt's early adulthood was a self-fulfilling prophecy: fishing proved as crucial to his success as it was to his happiness.

Eight

The Story of Sea World

On March 26, 1961, *The San Diego Union* ran a beguiling spread in the Sunday newspaper. A rare underwater photo showed a man in a diving mask floating among fishes. He appeared beneath the cryptic headline, "A Playground for Citizens of Land and Sea." The city would soon feature "an aquatic playground," the article explained, "where trained whales will perform, where sharks will race around a circular pool, where the public may watch and study other strange forms of marine life."

The news intrigued readers, for whom the sea held greater mystery than it does today. In 1961, neither *Flipper* nor *The Undersea World of Jacques Cousteau* had yet debuted. The earliest commercial SCUBA gear was an exotic luxury item. Gazing out to sea, most people could scarcely visualize what lay beneath its surface, even in a coastal community like San Diego. Trips to its world-famous zoo brought patrons face-to-face with animals from South America, Asia, and Africa. Most were less familiar with life indigenous to local shores: octopus, porpoises, eels, even tuna that wound up on their plates. Curiosity would draw them to an oceanarium, or so thought two rival groups of men competing for a lease to build the attraction.

The newspaper lavished far more display art and column inches on "Sealand," a proposal put forth by a team of local businessmen. Their concept would sprawl out over 70 acres of grounds, with huge pools surrounded by stadium seating, and even "an attempt to capture a deadly killer whale to swim with sharks in a large, doughnut-shaped ring." Today, the Sealand proposal reads like a portent of the orca shows that would come to define the marine park industry. In 1961, no one knew if sharks or killer whales could survive captivity let alone perform.

The enthusiastic write-up worried Milt, who belonged to the rival group of entrepreneurs. None of the four partners was a San Diego resident. Would their "Marine Park" concept get a fair hearing? They hadn't included anything as sensational as a killer whale chasing sharks—in fact, Marine Park had no plans to display an orca. If that was a mistake, it was too late to remedy. The four partners could only wait as the city reviewed their pitch. "A satisfactory lease could be drafted with either group," a municipal official had declared after poring over both proposals. "However, a choice must be made."

San Diego's desire for an oceanarium was more than two decades in the making. Once a sleepy community filled with retirees, it began to boom with the advent of World War II, when it was suddenly bursting with soldiers, sailors, and tens of thousands of defense workers, many in aerospace. After the war, many wanted to remain in the seaside city with its perfect climate. Officials who had spent half a decade scrambling to house workers faced a new challenge: with the end of the war economy, how would San Diego employ all its residents?

Hopeful that tourism would help, they decided to remake Mission Bay and the land around it into an aquatic reserve. New York City had Central Park, where visitors could stroll, bike, or picnic. San Diego would offer a seaside analog: 4,600 acres for sunbathing, kite-flying, sportfishing, sailing, and water-skiing. City leaders also sought to add an "all-seasons" attraction to draw visitors to the area year-round. Having watched the success of Walt Disney's Magic Kingdom, a theme park seemed a perfect fit. The San Diego Zoo already boasted a world-class collection of land animals. Perhaps its patrons would stay in town an extra day to see marine creatures.

The oceanarium concept traces back to Marine Studios, opened in 1938 near Jacksonville, Florida. Its founder, Cornelius Vanderbilt Whitney, admired the motion picture industry. Convinced that educators should mimic its approach to captivate young and old, he created "a cream-colored aquarium pitted with tempered glass portholes," as a WPA guide described it. "Each observer can sit comfortably in relative darkness," an early backer explained, "as if in a motion picture theater, looking out into a brilliant world of the undersea." Motion picture cameras were trained on the tanks too, a boon to biologists, who studied underwater animal behavior as never before, and to Hollywood, which used Marine Studios to film some of the earliest underwater scenes. In the 1950s, dolphin training began, and soon a bottle-nose named Flippy, the favorite performer at the facility, was cast in the big-budget film *Revenge of the Creature*. The dolphin's subsequent fame helped Marine Studios reinvent itself as Marineland, drawing a half-million annual visitors.

Imitators sprung up in Florida, and later on the West Coast. Officials in San Diego were particularly influenced by Marineland of the Pacific, an oceanarium that opened on August 28, 1954, on the Palos Verdes peninsula, just south of Santa Monica Bay. 14,000 gathered that first day for what one account called the largest collection of marine animals ever assembled.

As the novelty wore off the venture began to lose money, according to Jim Patryla's *A Photographic History Back to the Marineland of the Pacific*. In response, a new vice-president of operations was hired. He presided over a portentous shift: rather than just display animals like an aquarium, Marineland would entertain with scripted shows. In 1957, the oceanarium acquired a pilot whale, the first ever captured on the open ocean. Mr. Bimbo, the largest pilot whale in captivity, was added in 1959 and pushed attendance past 1 million visitors per year. Every ambitious city manager in the region took notice.

San Diego leaders felt that the concept could work even better at a larger scale on Mission Bay, and resolved to find the best entrepreneurs to build earth's most ambitious oceanarium. The project would complete Mission Bay Park. And San Diego would have an answer to Disneyland as Mickey Mouse drew tourists to Anaheim 100 miles to the north.

Fraternity Brothers Unite

The San Diego press dubbed Marine Park Corporation "a Long Beach syndicate," but the partnership is better described as a conspiracy of Bruins. All four members had belonged to the UCLA chapter of the Phi Kappa Sigma fraternity.

While acting as its alumni advisor, Milt had taken a liking to George Millay, a brash, red-headed freshman who had witnessed the attack on Pearl Harbor while growing up in Hawaii. In 1947, George followed his father into the Navy, where he forecast weather. At UCLA he majored in meteorology, but showed entrepreneurial ambitions too, buying a dump truck for $300, hiring classmates as cut-rate laborers, and pocketing enough in profits to expand his fleet. He lived a lifestyle that was the envy of his classmates. Drawn to his hard-charging personality, Milt became a mentor. "Don't be a weatherman," he advised his young friend. "Go into business."

George listened. He went to Long Beach in 1956 and became a stockbroker. "I had no customers, no clients. I didn't know my ass from third base," he said in *The Wave Maker*, his authorized biography. "But most of the guys didn't know anything. As long as you're one step ahead of the customer, you're doing all right."

Investing for others didn't satisfy George for long. In 1957, he raised $135,000 to open The Reef, a Hawaiian-themed bar and grill, earning a 10-percent stake for arranging the deal. He negotiated a $25,000 per-year salary, too, and spent a lot of nights there drinking free booze as a perk of part-ownership. Some nights, when friends dropped by, they would muse about business opportunities. One idea was especially intriguing to Milt: opening an underwater bar adjacent to the restaurant. The friends sketched out a vision. Patrons would pass down an acrylic tunnel into a submerged capsule, where they could watch fishes in the harbor and pay a premium for the pleasure. George went so far as to consult engineers.

They told him that the harbor water was too murky, that the presence of fish was too variable, that the construction costs were too great. Both men were disappointed. George loved to impress. Milt was eager to share his delight in fishes. And then, as Milt would tell it, "one night after a few too many beers we thought, why stop at a bar looking into the harbor?"

The core notion was that people would pay to see the underwater world. "We thought, why don't we start an oceanarium?"

Ken Norris already worked in the industry. An academic at heart, he would one day earn a master's degree in marine biology, a Ph.D. from the Scripps Institute of Oceanography, and accolades for his scientific research and scholarship. At the time, however, he was the head trainer at Marineland, where he trained dolphins and did pioneering research into echolocation. Had he been happy there, the partnership of Phi Kappa Sigmas might never have formed. But he felt Marineland could do more to entertain, educate, and advance marine biology, and his bosses wouldn't fund his ideas. How he longed to work at a place where his creativity and ambitions wouldn't be stymied! A scientist more than an entrepreneur, he mentioned to his friends that while he was happy to indulge their talk about an underwater bar, what he would really love is to consult for a state-of-the-art oceanarium. Had they heard that San Diego wanted to build one on Mission Bay?

Milt was eager to pursue the opportunity. He had already managed to entwine his life with the ocean as never before. His home on Kings Road was so close to the water that he could smell salt air from his driveway, and his client base was rife with recreational anglers. Joining them at sea was like skewering three fish with one spear: he kept up customer relations, met prospects in wealthy social circles, and fished in spots more advantageous than any he could reach on his own. If he had successfully turned fishing trips into business opportunities as a securities trader, an oceanarium would merge his professional life and his passion on the grandest scale. What could beat bringing the ocean to the masses for a living?

George had no interest in fish beyond a restaurateur's affinity for selling them. Yet he saw Disneyland spawning imitators and knew the depths of the ocean-themed amusement park had only begun to be plumbed. There was an opportunity to create something original. With an outsized ego and an uncanny ability to sell anything, George soon found himself as opinionated as Ken about what an ambitious oceanarium ought to be like. He wanted to build a first-class theme park that everyone would talk about and shell out lots of money to patronize, over and over again, for many years.

Ken had since left Marineland, but managed to secure its latest financials. Its attendance and profits were healthy. Thus reassured in their ambitions, the trio formed Marine Park Corporation, bringing aboard a fourth Phi Kappa Sigma, certified public accountant David DeMott, as their numbers cruncher.

The team was set.

And they called on yet another fraternity brother to advise them. Card Walker had taken a job in the mailroom at Walt Disney Productions in 1938. He would rise to vice president, joining the Board of Directors in 1960. If fraternal courtesy demanded that he indulge the questions of his fellow Phi Kappa Sigmas, he went above and beyond, introducing them to contacts throughout the company. He even permitted Disney employees to moonlight as Sea World consultants. E.D. Ettinger, Disney's Director of Public Relations, proved especially helpful, counseling Milt and George to commission a study outlining all aspects of the marine park business and listing what their pitch should address.

Any theme park that opened on Mission Bay in the early 1960s would enjoy several advantages. All five Southern California counties expected significant population growth, the University of California was set to open campuses at San Diego (1960) and Irvine (1965), and several major residential communities were being planned within an hour's drive. The site was also seconds away from a soon-to-open portion of Interstate 5, making it far more freeway-accessible than Marineland. Economic Research Associates forecast that by 1966, 1.1 million people would live within a 30-minute drive and 3.3 million people would live within two hours. A quarter of San Diego Zoo patrons traveled more than 200 miles to visit.

To proceed, Milt would have to commit tens of thousands of dollars to match what George had already invested, plus another $25,000 to help complete the feasibility study and proposal. He obsessed over the decision. With that sum, he could add on to his house, travel the world fishing, or better guard against a future depression. And if San Diego rejected their plan he would be left with mere words and drawings. Then again, he made good money, had secure clients, and would never find an opportunity better aligned with his passions. He studied every detail. He sought Peggie's counsel. Together, the couple took the biggest financial risk of their lives.

"Oceanarium Proposal, Mission Bay"

Aiming to win over a city with "world class" ambitions, Milt and his partners pushed themselves to consider what might be possible if roughly $2 million were spent on display tanks and marine mammal shows unlike any ever attempted. Some of their ideas would delight audiences three years later, on the drizzly morning when Sea World of San Diego welcomed its first guests. Others delighted on the page but would never exist. Thanks to the narrative section of their proposal, "A Visit to Marine Park," we can see their original vision and imagine patrons even at the attractions that would never be.

Let us join them, "a husband and wife in their middle 30s, together with their two children." Father, Mother, Sister, and Junior embodied a postwar trend: families with more time for recreation who spent it together, traveling on a new interstate highway system that permitted the middle class to venture farther from home. At the main gate they admiringly take in "the artistic effect of the buildings, the ample shade and rest areas," and a reflecting pool, where father suggests a snapshot.

Soon they descend to an underground amphitheater: 500 tiered seats that slope down to where a stage might be, but in its place is a darkened wall of aquarium glass as big as a cinema screen. The house lights are up. Intriguing shapes are just visible in the depths if the gathering crowd strains its eyes. "As they speculate, the grotto dims down just as the light level in the water increases," the Marine Park proposal states. "Then we see the first sensation—a body plunges through the water, trailing a necklace of silver-blue air bubbles." With the underwater world illuminated, the family is confronted with a smiling skin diver. And he makes an underwater bow! Amazingly, his voice fills the auditorium. He explains that he's able to speak thanks to a special underwater microphone in his diving mask, and adds that the amphitheater was built so his friends could entertain in the medium where their agility and beauty would be best appreciated.

Sister laughs as eight trained penguins arrive in formation, performing "underwater frills" that "display their grace in an underwater element, and with comic dignity delight their audience." Porpoises swim into the fantastical scene, where they "perform incredible and beautiful feats, including 'dancing' to the music of a popular ballet. They tow their trainer through an obstacle course and chase mechanical fish like greyhounds."

The family has scarcely stepped back into the sunlight when the roar of an engine sends Junior down a landscaped path. Deposited on a wooden dock, a sleek hydrofoil boat is before him:

> *Noting the make-up of the crowd, it's obvious that this is an attraction with high appeal for teenagers ... There's practically no water motion as you get underway. All you're conscious of is a feeling of skimming out over Perez Cove, the colorful shoreline of San Diego's beach area, the sunlight-bright friendly blue waters of this famous bay all combine to make a perfect setting for our adventure. Fellow passengers share your exhilaration as you tour at a leisurely pace. Now from the bridge the*

skipper announces he'll make two test speed runs down one of the world's most famous racing boat courses. He admonishes you to secure your hats. The engines surge towards full power, you're aware only of the wind sweeping by, there is no feeling of striking through the choppy water around you, the bow rises slightly as your speed increases. Your fellow passengers are now excitedly gripping the rails. Here and there a bright colored buoy flashes by.

After lunch, the family hurries to a show held on a large lagoon. Enclosed by lushly landscaped, sloping berms, "this enchanting setting is the location of the park's outdoor aquatic zoo." They sit beneath an acacia tree as the crowd hushes:

We note a young man poling a small gaily colored skiff from the shore out into the Lagoon. As he glides effortlessly over the surface, he introduces himself and points out the various features of the area and then proceeds to introduce us to his live "cast." He holds his throat mike to the surface of the water and three sea lions break the surface, barking into the mike as they acknowledge their individual introductions. He comments on the intelligence and unique characteristics of the California sea lion and advises us that these three, "Milt, George, and Dave," are really a three sea-lion-powered outboard engine, and their favorite sport—towing skiffs!

After affixing a tow rope to his friends he's off, "the three sea lions happily barking as they swim in unison around the lagoon while their human companion demonstrates balancing techniques on his 'sea lion' board." The era's corny humor comes through in the next passage. The trainer is described performing a difficult, one-footed pose: "The sea lions, hearing the applause, stop dead—and our 'startled' trainer takes a dunking, much to the delight of the audience. After recovering his composure and returning to the skiff, the trainer explains the 'accident,' claiming it's really professional jealousy on the sea lion's part."

And the show is only beginning. Porpoises race around the lagoon, the audience cheering as if at the horse track. Penguins wait at the finish line to declare a winner. For the finale, "repeated eight times daily," the trainer, back aboard his skiff, poles to the middle of the lagoon and summons its largest, heretofore-unseen resident: "Sniffles, a 20-foot pilot whale."

The improbable climax:

> *This behemoth of the deep appears and is introduced with a few facts... Then the Master of Ceremonies pats the beast on her "forehead" and steps unconcernedly from the boat to her back! Standing on her like a circus bareback rider, she begins to move slowly around the Lagoon until the trainer has her "heave to" for passengers—a troupe of delightful penguins who, on the approach of Sniffles, have lined up in orderly fashion on the shore line, and then swim out to "board" Sniffles. Their dignified appearance delights the audience and when, at the orders of their trainer, they line up for "vest inspection," delight turns to waves of laughter and*

applause. What follows is a wonderful display of their intelligence and adaptability as the Master of Ceremonies puts them through various "close order" military drills, right on the back of Sniffles, who meanwhile cruises slowly around the Lagoon, occasionally flicking her tail as though she meant to shoo these "flies" off her generous back. It was an impossible act to top and a fitting conclusion for a most unusual and fascinating show.

Still, the family seeks out a last attraction. As they descend underground, beads of moisture appear on an aquarium wall. They gaze through clear glass "into a beautifully reconstructed undersea reef," the proposal declares. "What a spectacle! Various unusual small fish of brilliant hues dart among the rocks, the coral settings, and forms of seaweed that grow luxuriantly." Enter a Javanese girl, Tina, "an attractive young lady clad in a Polynesian-designed swimsuit and carrying her scuba equipment." She'll conduct the tour underwater, she explains, while the group follows on the dry side of the glass.

At first, it seems as though Tina will swim from one display to the next. But she has no need to propel herself. "A huge green turtle shakes his flippers as Tina boosts herself gracefully aboard." Straddling the turtle's back as it swims, she describes various flora and fauna with easy expertise until it's time to dismount into a grotto, where tiny Gulf of California harbor porpoises are just the most conspicuous inhabitants. "We are introduced to all the creatures that inhabit our coastline," the proposal concludes. "We notice that we have gained in this tour through an underwater maze a completely new understanding and appreciation of Nature's sea creatures. Yet we had enjoyed one of the most entertaining experiences to be had."

It is time to depart, pausing only to buy a souvenir. Though more attractions remain, they will save them for another day, "a resolution well put by junior to his parents as we join them in leaving the park — 'Daddy, when can we come again, please?'"

The proposal was submitted in March. It weighed on Milt and Peggie through the beginning of June when L.E. Earnest, the director of Mission Bay Park, finally issued his recommendation. One group "appears to have gone into more extensive studies of the problem and design," he noted. Moreover, "this group appears to envision a higher use per acre, thereby requiring less than half as much land," and its organization includes "men with rich backgrounds in this field." Its feasibility studies were completed by "well-recognized firms," he added. "It is therefore recommended that the city enter into lease negotiations with Marine Park Corporation."

Milt's Time to Shine

The partners could scarcely celebrate: they had to amass $2 million, build a theme park, recruit staffers from accountants to zoologists, acquire a menagerie of marine creatures, and train them. Speed was vital to avoid missing the tourist season.

Milt was ideally suited to raise the capital. He had spent years steering clients to investments. He had never felt as much enthusiasm for a venture. His contacts skewed toward wealthy sea-lovers who spent their leisure time sportfishing, yachting and diving.

Who better to invest?

And Milt had an unusual reputation among these men: they regarded him as a winner and something of a visionary, a status that he had acquired over the course of the prior decade.

For sportfishermen of that era, there was no greater catch than the marlin, a prize billfish that stretches up to 11 feet, its back steely blue with lavender stripes, its belly silvery white. A skilled angler might catch a marlin in three days of trying or seek one for a week without success. Thus the astonishment one afternoon in 1952 when Milt and two friends, Dick Harrison and Walt Powelson, docked their vessel and unloaded five striped marlins. As writer Jan Fogt would explain in a *Marlin* magazine profile years later, Milt's innovations were integral to the haul. Back then, fishermen trolled for marlin with flying fish. But Milt noticed that he never found flying fish in marlin when gutting them. He devised an experiment: "He would fish for marlin using the fish he saw them feeding on."

Trolling with dead mackerel spooked the fish. But Milt kept observing his quarry. Nearly motionless before dawn, they spent late morning feeding near the surface. Rather than trolling at first light, like other fishermen, Milt decided to start his day catching mackerel so that he could use them as live bait later, when the marlin came alive. He would cast a still-living mackerel out near a striped marlin. "It's hard to understand what a radical theory this was at the time," Fogt wrote. Many peers considered trolling "the only sporting way to catch a marlin."

Milt "had specialized 10-foot-long custom casting rods made," Fogt explains. He would never forget the first time a marlin seized a live mackerel cast from his unusual gear. "We had this idea that everyone pretty much thought was crazy," he said. "So when it worked out so well, I admit, it made me feel good." Many had laughed at his unusually long rods. In the end, "Shedd was the only one laughing," Fogt wrote. "His rods became known throughout Southern California as Miltie Sticks."

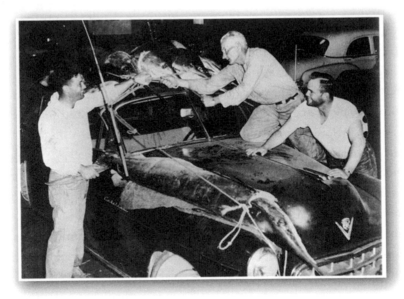

Herb Bell witnessed these triumphs. A prominent electronics entrepreneur who met Milt through his investment banking work, Bell would often invite Milt aboard his 98-foot yacht, *The Five Bells*, to indulge their shared love of angling. Their expeditions to Cabo San Lucas helped to turn the sleepy little port at the tip of Baja California into a sportfishing mecca. Over the years, Bell watched his friend succeed enough times on the ocean to surmise that he would approach the oceanarium business with the same meticulous preparation, intensity, and creativity. In 1963, he became an early investor. Having so prominent a businessman on board helped legitimize the business, renamed Sea World on a Disney consultant's advice.

To that point, Milt had never entered a sportfishing tournament. He always felt himself to be in competition with the fish, not other fishermen. Playing to his strengths, he made an exception that year, forming a team for the Hawaii International Billfish Tournament, perhaps the world's most prestigious. His team won, the first ever from California to do so. And some of the team members went on to invest in Sea World.

Back in San Diego, corporate underwriters were signing on. Hawaiian Punch sponsored a pavilion where guests would order nonalcoholic, Polynesian-themed drinks and look out at Mission Bay. The Murata Pearl Company of Tokyo committed to build a Japanese-themed pavilion, though its CEO was a former Japanese general and Sea World's partners were all military veterans. Thanks to George Millay, Sea World's builders would have skin in the game too. Moffatt and Nichol, the engineering firm that nixed the underwater bar concept, invested $250,000. And the architectural firm that did much of Sea World's original design work invested $35,000.

Together, the partners had raised more than $1 million—well short of their target. "Our loans were all dependent on getting a specific amount of equity," George said in his biography. "I was worried. Shedd was tapped out and I didn't know what to do." But Milt wasn't tapped out. Once again, he called on a Phi Kappa Sigma. UCLA alum Jeff Ascher was an employee of Boston Capital. "Miltie was a forceful personality—trustworthy, persuasive, an evident leader," he recalled. "I took his proposal to my board and we put up half-a-million dollars so they would have the wherewithal to succeed." That stake soon doubled. Boston Capital was a $1 million investor.

Building the Oceanarium

Now all four partners could get to work. Milt would serve as Sea World's Chairman of the Board, overseeing the whole enterprise. Davey DeMott remained the numbers man. As SeaWorld's first president, George began his tenure finalizing its layout and attractions and overseeing construction. He would credit a team led by Ben Southland with designing and building "the ponds, the flowing rivers, waterfalls, and rock work, the elements for which Sea World of San Diego is famous."

Ken Norris' role was the most complicated. Hoping to apply his expertise to several marine parks in different regions, he founded his own company, Aquatic Consultants. "As a consulting firm specializing in tank and display designs, specimens capture, transport, care and associated problems, we agree to devote as much time as is necessary... prior to the opening of the facilities," its contract with Sea World stated. The company would install filtration and pumping systems, develop animal shows, recruit and train staff, collect specimens, and visit the construction site as necessary to lend assistance.

But even as workers began assembling aquariums, digging out a lagoon, and building aquatic stadiums, and before Ken had collected fish, acquired marine mammals, scripted animal shows, or designed programs for animal training, he was offered a professorship at UCLA. The chance to be a tenured biologist would have been tempting under any circumstances. And as work on Sea World proceeded, Ken found that George wanted creative control, even though he had no experience in the industry. With some of his designs stymied, Ken couldn't help but imagine a future at Sea World as frustrating as his Marineland past. For his part, George felt that Ken was insufficiently invested in Sea World; that Ken ought to defer on business questions; and that Ken's proper role was collecting and training Sea World's marine creatures, not being the marine park's visionary, a role George wanted for himself.

Milt, an expert at conciliation, managed to keep them cooperating for awhile and ensured that their squabbling didn't jeopardize the project. As he later reflected, "There is a pecking order among all living creatures—people behave just like chickens in that sense—and I've always felt my role in business was to understand this pecking order and help people work effectively." As tensions grew, one man had to go. And there was no doubt about who was higher in the pecking order.

"I, Kenneth S. Norris, acknowledge that I have committed myself to many ventures which have been going on simultaneously with early operation of Sea World," a severance agreement stated. "I have been unable to match the efforts and time contributed by each of the other three principals." The company bought back his stock for $1,250. He would go on to be a renowned marine biologist and to contribute to several oceanariums, mostly in Hawaii. "I, George D. Millay, acknowledge that I have been hostile toward Kenneth S. Norris, both personally and business-wise," the agreement added. George pledged that he would "make no derogatory comments concerning his character or capabilities."

Jeff Ascher, who kept close tabs on Sea World on behalf of Boston Capital, hated to see his friend Ken's departure. "It was a shame, because George was a visionary when it came to any type of theme park, but wasn't particularly interested in fish," he said. "Ken was a visionary in just that one area. He had a more sophisticated vision of what an oceanarium might achieve, but he didn't have as strong a personality, and ultimately only one of them could be calling the shots." A disappointed Ascher helped to negotiate Ken's buyout, but retained his faith in Sea World. "Milt and George were the only two where, without both, you never could've made it happen," he said. "Milt gave the perspicacious strength and stability without which George would've screwed up the works. He was the center pin that made the thing go. Without Milt, I don't think you could've had it. Without George, you couldn't have it either. He was the promoter, the dreamer."

Catch and Transport

Sea World suddenly needed a new plan to acquire marine creatures, having lost the partner who had intended to gather many of them on collecting trips off California's coast and longer expeditions to fertile fishing grounds near Cabo San Lucas.

Milt filled the breach. He couldn't claim Ken's oceanarium experience or academic background. But he had spent many weeks fishing off Baja, had observed the species found in Mexican waters, had hired locals as deck hands, and knew the Mexican government's permitting requirements. He had even done his share of diving with some of the earliest SCUBA gear. He began corresponding with Mexican contacts to set up a collecting program. When all was prepared, he would lead a small team charged with gathering the needed specimens.

The task was as novel a logistical challenge as he had faced since the war. There would be equipment to transport, skiffs to build on site, a section of lagoon to net off as a holding pen for fishes, and Mexican workers to train in unusual fishing techniques. His friendship with Herb Bell once again came in handy: Sea World would be permitted free use of *The 5 Bells* as its base of operations. Milt would send the boat ahead, fly down to meet it, collect sea creatures, and return home by plane. The itinerary, repeated several times over several months, allowed him to continue his Chairman of the Board duties and to avoid long stretches away from his family.

Collecting sea creatures proved much more difficult than recreational fishing. Everything had to be kept alive. And for species not typically targeted by anglers, merely figuring out the best method of capture was a process of fisherman's intuition mixed with trial-and-error. "Dad's basic philosophy on those trips was the same as always," his son Bill explained. "You look at how things happened in the past, forget what everybody says about what you can and cannot do, and figure out how to do something unique and different that just might work."

Tales of that first expedition would reach the ears of David Powell, later hired as Sea World's curator of fishes. He recounted some of the most vivid anecdotes in his engrossing memoir, *A Fascination with Fish*. "The best was a description of Milt Shedd... sitting on the bottom in scuba gear trying to catch Moorish idols with a tiny rod, reel, and minute baited hook," he wrote. "Moorish idols, of course, graze on tiny animals and algae that encrust the rocks. While he didn't actually catch any, he certainly won the prize for effort."

More often, the team got their quarry. They started out diving by day, sucking all manner of tropical fish into slurp guns. There were risks in the operation. Once, while Milt was free diving, a big grouper appeared. As it swam past, he noticed it had a heavy line attached to it, having escaped an unknown angler. Curious, he grabbed hold, enjoying the tow but misjudging the speed of the fish's descent. Around 35 feet down his ear drum burst. More alarming than the pain was his loss of equilibrium: he couldn't discern which way was up or down. Squelching panic, he had the presence of mind to blow bubbles, watch them rise, and follow them back to the surface.

Nighttime dives were riskier still. Slipping off the boat, they would enter shark-infested waters carrying little more than a dive light that would illuminate a small area around them, leaving them visible yet blind to the surrounding darkness. But the team had discovered that butterfly fishes, angelfishes, parrotfishes, and Moorish idols are difficult to catch in daylight. "The absolute rule was this: we were together in the boat before the dive and we were together in the boat after the dive," Powell wrote, describing protocol he inherited when taking over the trips. "In the water, we pretty much went our own way. Sticking together would have cut our catch rate considerably. We would have wasted time looking for our buddy in the dark instead of concentrating on catching fish."

The collecting method demanded concentration. "We each carried a small mesh-nylon hand net, a plastic bag under the crotch strap of our wet suit, a dive light, and a number of different-sized hypodermic needles tucked under the wrist cuff of our wet suit," Powell explained. "The hypodermic needles were to release the expanding air from the swim-bladder. If you shine the dive light right into the eye of the chosen fish, it can usually be netted quickly with a flip of the wrist."

Then came the hard part, done in near darkness:

The job is to get it out of the net and into the plastic bag tucked under your crotch strap. The dive light is held between your legs while the bag is pulled out from your suit. Grasping the fish in the netting, you invert it into the bag and shake it loose, without letting any already collected fish escape… the light between your legs keeps you from kicking. If your buoyancy is a little negative, there's the risk of sinking down on an unseen patch of needle-sharp sea urchins.

Dives were timed to minimize moonlight. "Sometimes we'd go out at three in the morning and finish just at first light," he recalled. But fishes collected and put into netted-off receivers in a lagoon had to be fed every day thereafter. As the captive population grew, the schedule of diving late at night and resting during the day morphed into 24-hour periods of almost constant work: the team acquired creatures to display at Sea World by night, then spent days fishing for species that could be ground up into food to keep the captives alive. The team would be exhausted. But Milt later called those days and nights of near constant fishing the best time of his life.

Before flying home, he would try to arrange for the cheap transport of their specimens. "There was a fleet out of San Diego that would go to Central America to fish," Bill explained. "When they stopped in Cabo San Lucas to refuel before going back to San Diego, dad would convince them to fill their empty bait tanks with whatever he had ready to transport. He'd say that he didn't have to pay those guys a cent, 'not even a pack of cigarettes.' Dad had a lot of fishermen friends, and they were fascinated by this park that was being built."

The Five Bells filled its own bait tanks to capacity when it finally returned north. The first trip proved frustrating, for many of the tropical fish died en route while passing through colder waters. Milt prevailed on his friend Herb Bell to make a small modification to the vessel for subsequent trips, so that the bait tanks could be warmed. "It consisted of periodically sticking a thermometer in the holding-tank water and then adjusting a valve by hand—and hoping it was right," Powell wrote. "On the earlier trip, the fish merely ran the risk of dying from the cold. Now we had the added possibility of cooking them."

Odds and Ends in San Diego

George was busy hiring a staff, including "Sea Maids," young women trained in SCUBA and cast in early shows. Described in promotional material as "the glamorous stars of Sea World," they were "19 to 23 years old, from 5 feet 2 inches to 5 feet 8 inches tall. They are 'everything you'd expect a pretty girl to be'—except married, which is against the rules."

Milt applied himself to any number of tasks: he wrote his friend Bobby Tidwell in Papeete, Tahiti, asking him to ship pieces of coral for use in Sea World display tanks; he met with Santa Fe Railroad representatives on Sea World's behalf; he watched the first porpoises training in Sea World's just-finished display pool; and he wrote George to comment on a candidate for a marketing job after worrying that his colleague had rejected a strong applicant too early in the process. Milt constantly provided that sort of oversight. And George was as frequently annoyed that a man with a personality as forceful as his own was overseeing his actions. Often, Milt agreed with George's judgment, or else deferred to it, knowing that he could only impinge so far on his partner's independence if he hoped to extract his full potential. But Milt also had a way of inserting himself into important matters.

In August 1963, George was arranging to buy several beluga whales from a sportsman's club that was to deliver them to an Alaska airport for $500 per animal. Granting that the price was low, Milt worried that his partner had not done enough to hedge their bets. What if the sportsmen delivered an unacceptable whale to the costly charter plane that would have to be waiting? What if they found that catching beluga whales was more difficult than a $500 payday justified? As Milt saw it, "Enthusiasm rather than sound practical business considerations more often than not prompts a group like this sportsman's club to take on such an activity," and by relying on them, Sea World was minimizing its upfront costs at too great a risk.

"If we do not mount and lead this entire expedition utilizing the sportsman's club to best advantage," he wrote, "we should at least have a capable operator accompanying and assisting them… We lose little by assuming they will not produce or that serious misunderstandings will develop and that we must have our own man on the scene to finish the job or at least prevent delays. A $1000 or $2000 expenditure to have our man participating is cheap insurance in relation to the values Sea World would gain from a successful Beluga display."

Milt's most serious concerns were expressed in a December 14, 1963, letter that captures how he would set forth George's weaknesses when he deemed it a necessity. After praising his partner's drive, imagination, and dedication, Milt suggested that he made a better president than a general manager, and needed to hire for the latter position rather than running things in patchwork fashion with peculiar divisions of authority.

He wrote:

> "With all the 'experts' and specialized talent working at Sea World, one of our management's most important responsibilities has to be that of personnel management, of getting the best out of these people. We must make that organization chart function on site just as you show it functioning on paper. With the technical people, the sensitive personalities on whom we must rely at the working level, this will be no mean task and one that you'll agree that you are not going to do effectively. As you said a dozen times, you really don't understand these people.
>
> The man charged with making this chain of command function must be given authority to develop his own techniques, his own approaches and his own methods… He must develop efficient, routine ways of passing on instructions to his workers, collecting suggestions from them, granting pay raises or promotions, and giving out commendations… In the process many delicate and sensitive relations will be built up between these people. This man can never do a good job functioning as your lackey. Your personality must be kept in the background. You, George, have absolutely no idea the effect that you have on this chain of command relationship when you charge out of your president's chair like the proverbial bull in a china shop."

The general manager "can't be your puppet," Milt continued, and must be a strong enough presence "to tell you to get back to your president's chair when he feels you are interfering." He concluded that with Sea World just months away from opening, the problem had to be solved. "In no way should this letter be construed as a commentary on the suitability of any of the people you have hired," he wrote. "It concerns what you as our president are going to do to meet a serious problem, the seriousness of which I'm convinced has escaped you."

The Race to Opening Day

An illustrated brochure sat atop Milt's desk. Were these the first images that Sea World wanted to put before the public? The cover shows a young woman with auburn hair and an orange swimsuit standing on a platform in the middle of a lagoon. Her arms are aloft in a V-shape. A rope encircles her waist. She is towed forward by two dolphins leaping a foot or so out of the water, their torsos encircled by leis. All are overshadowed by a third dolphin soaring over the woman's head at the apex of a magnificent leap. "Enter a dazzling underwater kingdom," the brochure declares. "Here you discover the most unusual entertainment attraction that this country has seen in years..." The sights at Sea World "are brighter, livelier, lovelier than any you have seen," the text boasted. Carefully chosen words, no doubt. But Milt knew that the most consequential copy was in tiny print at the bottom:

"Sea World Opens March 21, 1964."

Customers would line up that morning expecting something special. They wouldn't find the Marine Park described in the pitch to San Diego. There would be no Great Barrier Reef exhibit, no Javanese guide named Tina, no penguins lining up on a whale's back. But there would be plenty to impress a young family that had never gone fishing or snorkeling or diving. They could begin their day in the Theater of the Sea, watching Sea Maids dive behind giant picture windows. And how could they fail to be entertained by "the world's first underwater productions written for and starring... Dolphins!" It would be staged underwater in a 160,000-gallon tank.

Early ads touted non-marine attractions, too. Sea World would compete with amusement parks for the affection of children, even as it focused on its comparative advantage as an ocean aquarium. The dual nature of the

95

enterprise mirrored the differences of its founders. Milt was driven largely by his passion for the ocean. He knew the wonder and delight that marine life evoked in himself, delighted in bringing that feeling to others, and believed that success would depend on exploiting and stoking natural interest in the sea. As he would tell stockholders, "Your investment in SeaWorld is a means by which you can participate in the public's ever-growing fascination and curiosity about the marine environment." Adventure rides and scripted animal shows might be necessary to stay competitive with Disneyland and Marineland, but would never be sufficient if Sea World was to thrive as a business or fulfill its social mission.

For George, the appeal of marine creatures to the public was evident; but they weren't his passion or even his priority. Permitted to trade places with Jacques Cousteau or P.T. Barnum, his choice would be easy; while running the three-ring circus, he would open a theme-restaurant-and-bar next door. He took particular pleasure in the hydrofoils, which were a part of the oceanarium on opening day; the Hawaiian Punch Village, featuring color travel films from the South Pacific; and the Murata Pearl Company pavilion, a showcase of Japanese architecture, dress, and ritual where women from Japan would dive to the bottom of a deep, clear pool, retrieve oysters, and open them for patrons who would buy the harvested pearls.

Welcome to Sea World

The grand opening took place on March 21, 1964, as promised. "In spite of the cold, wet conditions, a 14-year-old camped out under the main gate arch, determined to be Sea World's first visitor," an internal company newsletter reported. Patrons filtered into the parking lot throughout the morning, bypassing a picket line formed to protest non-union labor. Admission was $2.25 for adults, $1.25 for juniors, and $.75 cents for children. Davey himself took tickets at the front gate. Inside, Sea World's 44 full-time employees and 150 part-timers were excited, nervous, and doing their harried best.

A gardener showed up in a suit and tie, not realizing there were no uniforms yet. He pulled weeds and dug ditches in his Sunday best, then helped the hospitality staff to sell popcorn and wash dishes. Management had its own problems. The grand opening would feature appearances by Barry Goldwater, who was in the midst of his presidential run, and Art Linkletter, a radio and TV personality. To spare the dignitaries from having to cross a picket line, Sea World brought them in from Mission Bay aboard the Bahia Bell, a Victorian-style paddle wheeler. At first, it made for a grand spectacle: En route, water-skiers wearing shirts emblazoned with AuH20, the symbols for gold and water, crisscrossed in front of the boat. But a smaller raft was needed to get Goldwater and his wife to the center of the dolphin lagoon for the dedication ceremony. And as Milt and Peggie accompanied them, the small craft began to flounder. "We barely made it off without getting wet," Peggie said. "What a disaster, that whole day," she continued. "Later, all the toilets overflowed and the plumbing started backing up into the lagoon."

The facilities staff was already overwhelmed, for when the Bahia Belle dropped off its dignitaries, its paddles stirred up mud on the bottom of Mission Bay, clogging the park's intake filters. Suddenly, the Sea Maids were barely visible in their underwater show. As George later explained, Sea World had the means to handle "primary water, mammal water, fresh water, chilled water, heated water, and recycled water," but the staff didn't entirely understand the system, and were stymied by a series of red tides before opening day. The tiny microorganisms clogged filters and made water drawn into the park appear brown and dirty. Stirring up sediment near the intake filters made poor water clarity even worse. "Visibility was nil," George's biography states. "Art Linkletter looked in, smiled and said, 'Look George, I'll come back some other time.'"

Due in part to Ken's untimely departure, the oceanarium opened with just two scripted shows. In one, held in the outdoor dolphin lagoon, "Jim, a pilot who crash lands on a desert island, is greeted by dolphins who leap, dive, and splash about. But the story has a happy ending, with dolphins presenting a beautiful native girl to Jim." The other show, held in the indoor Theater of the Sea, was "the tale of a sailor who pollutes a small cove where his boat is anchored. After he tosses litter into the water, dolphins become annoyed and sink him. Diving beneath the water to retrieve his boat, the sailor sees the happy life there and is so impressed that he resolves to abide by the standards of dolphins and Sea Maids." George later said the earliest animal shows were mediocre, "but in general, people like animals no matter what they do, and the park got away with much more than it could today."

As Sea World ended its first day of operations, Milt, George, and Davey were relieved that it was over, chagrined by their failures, and uncertain about how they would be received. They had anticipated 10,000 patrons, but only 4,000 had come, due in part to the morning rain, they guessed. Confident that Sea World could improve with time, they hoped that the opening day reviews wouldn't cost them future visitors. They would be kept in suspense overnight. The next morning, the first verdict arrived in the pages of the *San Diego Union*:

> *Sea World Is a Wonderland*
>
> *San Diego's wonderful world of spectator attractions has been expanded tremendously by the addition of Sea World, the multimillion dollar extravaganza in Mission Bay Park. Sea World is a Wonderland as fascinating as that visited by the fictional Alice. We can make statements such as that without feeling they are tinged by San Diego partisanship. Newsmen from all sections of the state who attended a preview of Sea World's wonders said, in effect, "greatest show about the sea on earth." Sea World complements San Diego's other great attractions such as the zoo, beaches, fishing opportunities, and dozens of historical points. The shows exhibited there, even when they were initially revealed, are examples of what can be accomplished by skilled, professional direction. Sea World, we predict, is destined to become one of the nation's outstanding attractions.*

For all that the partners had fretted, their most important review suggested that the public would look past imperfections for a while. Sea World would keep striving for all its dolphins to hit all their cues in crystal clear water. But if they started out with most dolphins hitting most cues in murky water, visitors who had never seen the creatures up close would leave happy. George was confident that new hires in maintenance and animal training would improve the park within months. In fact, in an October 1964 letter to stockholders, Sea World management announced that it would close on Mondays and Tuesdays for the duration of the winter to allow extra time for training animals and refining shows.

Milt worked to resolve a problem with the Murata Pearl Village. Patrons loved their visits. But Sea World's agreement with the Murata Pearl Company allowed it to charge an extra admission fee, which proved wildly unpopular: after buying tickets to enter the park, many resented discovering that they would have to pay again for an advertised attraction. To end the single biggest complaint of otherwise forgiving patrons, Sea World unilaterally altered the agreement, setting aside a portion of general admissions, calculated at $28,000, to reimburse Murata Pearl Company for letting everyone into their attraction for free.

As 1965 began, Sea World was missing its targets. It had hoped to draw a fifth of the San Diego Zoo's attendance, for example, but was drawing just 13 percent. "We were virtually unknown in the Los Angeles area," a letter to stockholders later stated. "To make matters worse, the San Diego population was not supporting us as strongly as we had hoped." In ensuing months, Sea World improved its animal shows by hiring a new department head and got freelance help from Disney scriptwriters. And a Beverly Hills ad agency crafted a series of TV spots depicting a young boy named Bobby and his fantastic day there. The oceanarium wound up beating the previous year's attendance by 58 percent and achieved net earnings, though it remained $324,000 in debt. Was it improved enough to survive? The world shall never know, for in the last weeks of 1965, Sea World acquired a new star that forever changed its course.

A Killer Turnaround: Shamu

For Americans who grew up cheering "Save the Whales" campaigns and cuddling Orca stuffed animals, pre-1960s attitudes toward killer whales are hard to fathom. The creatures elicited awe and fear at their perceived savagery but little sympathy or affection. During the 1940s, the U.S. and Canadian air forces used pods of orcas as targets to practice bombing raids. Fishermen in the 1950s would shoot the not-yet-iconic mammals. "In 1960, private fishing lodges on Vancouver Island persuaded the Canadian government to install a machine gun at Campbell River to cull the orca population," David Kirby wrote in his history of killer whales in captivity.

The machine gun was never fired. A historic shift in attitudes toward orcas began in the early 1960s, driven by unprecedented contact with the creatures. Within the decade, a species never before taken captive would endear themselves to millions while performing at Sea World. But the oceanarium was not the first enterprise to display a killer whale in captivity, and it would not have played the biggest part in popularizing the creatures but for several accidents of history.

The first orca taken for display was captured in 1962 while disoriented among the boat slips in Newport Harbor. A team from Marineland of the Pacific was alerted to the whale's presence, and Frank Brocato, who had previously taken pilot and beluga whales for the oceanarium, managed to lift it from the water and truck it to Palos Verdes. It died two days later.

New attempts to display an orca for the public seemed inevitable—those San Diego businessmen who dreamt of a killer whale chasing a shark were hardly alone in seeing their commercial potential—yet none would be taken captive again until 1964, and that was a fluke. A sculptor named Samuel Burich was hired to kill an orca so that its carcass could be displayed in a new hall at the aquarium in Vancouver, British Columbia. To carry out that commission, he chartered a boat, harpooned a killer whale, and fired several bullets into its flank.

But the orca didn't die. The panicked sculptor used a ship-to-shore radio to relay that information to Murray Newman, the aquarium director who had hired him. And Newman decided that the wounded creature should be spared. Dubbed Moby Doll, the killer whale was towed for 16 hours to a temporary pen in Vancouver. Discovered to be male after 87 days, his seemingly tame demeanor challenged the prevailing assumption that orcas were vicious, aggressive creatures. He became a celebrity thanks to press reports and public intrigue, even as scientists flocked to his pen to record his vocalizations.

Enter Ted Griffin, owner of the Seattle Marine Aquarium. Enamored by killer whales, he had spent months trying to capture one with a tranquilizer gun, shooting darts from a boat and later a helicopter. In 1965, a local fisherman aware of his obsession found an orca tangled in his salmon net and saw an opportunity. Griffin agreed to pay $8,000 for the creature. He named the killer whale Namu, towed him to Seattle in a custom cage, and kept him in an aquatic pen at Rich Cove, where tens of thousands of people came to see the whale.

The potential to profit off an orca was more obvious than ever. But Griffin's initial plan for his prize was more personal. "From our first meeting in the swirling tidal waters of British Columbia, I began to prepare myself for swimming with Namu," he wrote. "I wanted to know this animal as intimately as a human could. Really close contact was possible only in the whale's medium—the sea. In the water, I would be relatively helpless. To be safe, I would have to be completely accepted by the animal. I must get him used to my presence, even to count on it."

Griffin began spending hours with the whale on the catwalk that surrounded his pen. Next he took to a small rowboat, then a rubber raft. Namu then permitted himself to be pet by his captor. And that August, Griffin became the first human to swim with a captive orca. "Was I frightened? Yes — plenty!" he wrote. "But optimistic as well, and too busy to get panicky."

His boldness was rewarded. "I slid onto his back and tugged gently at his huge dorsal fin," he wrote. "He swam two or three times around the pen with his unfamiliar burden, then bucked me off as if with a shrug... From then on it was a honeymoon."

Well, not quite. Believing Namu to be lonely, he resolved to find him a companion. With a partner, Don Goldsberry, he managed to trap 15 orcas in a nearby inlet and isolated the most promising, a young, 2,000-pound female that they dubbed "She-Namu" and called Shamu. "I am convinced that Namu, Shamu, and their kind can be trained to match the agility and adroitness of dolphins in tricks involving controlled leaps," he predicted. "But anyone working with a killer whale must realize that this is a dangerous, unpredictable creature. Its intelligence can be both a reassurance and a threat."

Shamu quickly proved too young to mate and no less costly to feed. To cut expenses, Griffin decided to try leasing the female orca to an aquarium or oceanarium. Sea World officials proposed an outright sale. The ensuing transfer was an awesome public spectacle: on Monday, December 20, 1965, Shamu became the first orca in history to fly. A chartered cargo jet took her to San Diego, where a crane and flatbed truck awaited. The *Los Angeles Times* reported that "the baby whale, whose breed has long been dreaded by mariners because of its ferocity, was taken to the Sea World oceanarium and hoisted into a training tank." A new era had begun.

Shamu started in a 45-foot-by-20-foot tank beside a dolphin named George put there to keep her company. On the third day, Kent Burgess, Sea World's head trainer, warily entered her enclosure for the first time. "I swam directly towards Shamu," he wrote in a work journal. "She put her head against me and pushed me towards the platform. She didn't seem vicious at all, but acted gently as if she were playing or wanted to be petted."

Shamu's mere presence was a draw. Patrons crowded her tank just to watch her train. It took two months for the orca to perform her first trick, touching her rostrum to a pole 10 feet in the air. Even Milt, who had seen orcas leap in the wild, loved to see it performed. But Sea World knew from past experience with its dolphins and sea lions that the novelty of so simple a feat wouldn't last. They would need to feature Shamu in choreographed shows with entertaining scripts to please the public.

Given the reputation of killer whales, it's easy to imagine Shamu being cast as a ruthless predator, perhaps opposite a trainer who acted like a lion tamer to a lioness. Instead, the orca was anthropomorphized from the start. The first known Sea World scripts cast her as a patient and her trainer as a doctor who examines her belly, checks her reflexes, and peers into her throat with a giant tongue depressor. In a crowd-pleasing addition, a giant toothbrush was used to polish her smile. She even learned to pop up to give her "doctor" a thank you kiss.

Anticipating that 1966 would be Sea World's biggest summer yet, Milt signed off on a 1,500-seat penguin and seal arena, a new snack bar, more restrooms, new holding pens for the dolphin lagoon, and a new script for the Theater of the Sea. New corporate sponsorships from Lockheed Aircraft Corporation, Royal Crown Cola and Foremost Dairies helped to defray the costs. George lobbied for even more aggressive spending, while Milt insisted on slower growth with a bigger margin for error.

His biggest worry was the precariousness of relying on a single living creature as Sea World's premier attraction, a concern that only intensified after July of 1966, when news came that Namu had died. Even as Kent Burgess trained Shamu, Milt directed him to coordinate with marine biologists who sought to research the creature, especially while she was briefly the only orca in captivity. Her blood was drawn; air expelled from her blowhole was analyzed; her metabolism was studied; her heart and breathing rates were tracked. As Milt saw it, these scientific inquiries were inherently valuable—he was fascinated by the data—and in harmony with business imperatives. Better understanding killer whales could only assist in successfully keeping them alive and healthy.

Author Lou Jacobs Jr., related one early health challenge in the earliest book on the not-quite-famous Shamu, which was published in 1967. The orca strongly preferred salmon, the fish to which she was accustom, to the bonito and mackerel more easily found in San Diego. While weaning her, the training team made too abrupt a transition, causing the whale to refuse all food. The next attempt proceeded more slowly, and in time, Shamu grew so used to bonito and mackerel that she refused salmon offered as a treat, according to Jacobs. His book illustrates how quickly attitudes about killer whales were changing. Considered fearsome beasts just a few years prior, Jacobs believed that Shamu posed little threat to her minders. "Perhaps a large group of killer whales in captivity might attack humans if they were hungry, but a single orca, well fed, healthy, and presumably happy, becomes a pet," he declared.

Google, a 2,000-pound elephant seal, posed a bigger threat to handlers, he argued, having lunged at them and even leapt fences to escape their control. "When maintenance men wash the insides of the windows above Shamu's tank, she may play with them, and even take a man's foot and leg in her mouth. But she does not bite, nor does she mean any harm," he wrote. "These men are almost strangers to her, but they are safe. At times one of them will shoot a stream of water at Shamu from a hose. She opens her mouth and plays around like a child."

Now the killer whale show was on a fixed schedule: held six times daily, it was the marine park's biggest draw; and while Shamu still missed her cues, the crowds didn't mind as long as new tricks were added. "Burgess was first to try what seemed like a dangerous stunt, but it turned out," Jacobs speculated, "that Shamu enjoys carrying a man around the tank, speeding to catch the pieces of fish he throws out ahead to urge her on."

Sea World had made it by the end of 1967. If its future wasn't assured, its prospects were bright enough for Milt to decide that investing in long-term growth was the prudent course. The oceanarium's most important acquisition that year was more killer whales. In a 1968 expedition, Griffin captured an entire pod in Yukon Harbor, corralling 15 orcas into a purse seine at sunset. The next morning, seven were let go. Three were towed to Seattle Marine Aquarium. Three died during the roundup. And two males, Ramu and Kilroy, were sold to Sea World.

Along with two new performers, Sea World had acquired a source of sperm. A breeding program now loomed in its future. As if to portend the need for it, Griffin and Goldsberry began to attract public criticism for their orca roundups.

"Is the chasing of killer whales in our local waters legal? Ethical? Humane?" wrote Dr. Victor Scheffer, a Marine Mammal Biologist at the Bureau of Commercial Fisheries, Seattle. "Since 1965, six whales have admittedly been killed by Seattle showmen," he complained. "Many others have been quietly killed or mortally wounded by harpoons, drug syringes, and nets. No laws of any kind protect the smaller cetaceans of North America. Should individuals have the right to harass and maim wild animals which belong to all residents of the Pacific Northwest? The highly integrated social behavior and intelligence of this mammal will allow him to learn through experience, sensitized by the bloodshed of his fellows, to avoid areas of known danger. Must we all lose the thrill of seeing these magnificent beasts free, unalarmed and approachable because individuals seek profit or fame?"

To Milt, profiting from killer whales and exposing them to the public were complementary undertakings. Sea World netted $1.37 million in the first three quarters of 1968 by attracting more than 1 million visitors. Shamu was easily the biggest draw, assuring that the park would survive to expose millions more who would never venture onto the ocean to its most magnificent creatures. With Shamu's star rising, Sea World went public. Milt was ecstatic: having touted Sea World to its earliest backers, including close friends, he was relieved to have done well by them, as well as by his own family. And he never wavered from the conviction that Sea World benefitted humanity.

He perceived a virtuous circle. Sea World attractions stoked public interest in the marine environment. That increased public support for conservation, research, and exploration, prompting discoveries that would inspire even more interest, creating new customers for Sea World. "What we are doing is not meant solely to entertain," he said in a 1968 speech. "We are attempting to enlighten the public into understanding and appreciating the marine environment. In this way, we believe we will not only be performing an important public function but will be increasing the potential for future growth."

Milt spent 1969 overseeing Sea World's preparations for the future. With more cash on hand than ever before, management built a 320-foot sky tower at the San Diego park; added Kandu, a 6-year-old female, to its collection of orcas; and invested the bulk of its resources in a momentous new venture. Sea World Ohio opened on May 29, 1970, for its first season on Geauga Lake, near Cleveland. Guests saw something they could scarcely imagine a few years prior: an orca performing in their Midwestern city! Sea World managed to arrange air transportation for an array of marine mammals, flying them east each spring and back to San Diego in early autumn, long before the first freeze. Despite its seasonal operations, bringing the ocean to the heartland proved even more successful than management had imagined. As the next annual report to stockholders put it, "1970 was a banner year in attendance and profit for our company. Ohio turnstiles clicked off 944,457 paid admissions, 51 percent more than projected."

Net profits were up 92 percent.

In the spring of 1971, the San Diego park left little doubt as to its strategy, debuting a 3,000 seat, million-gallon killer whale stadium and an equally telling new script, titled Shamu Goes to Hollywood. "From a little known whale five years ago, this animal is now 'producer, director and star' of her own show, lives in a $1.5 million home and is the idol of millions," a promotion declared. "You have come a long way, Shamu."

That same year, Walt Disney World opened in Florida, guaranteeing that Orlando would be a family tourism destination. Sea World quickly acquired 175 acres nearby. Operating three oceanariums, even as Sea World branded Shamu its shining star, would create more pressure than ever to assure a supply of killer whales, a business imperative that was growing more difficult. In 1970, Don Goldsberry and Ted Griffin had executed their most controversial orca roundup yet: they trapped 80 killer whales with a net near Penn Cove, Washington, chose the seven youngest to sell, and negligently drowned several orcas. Hoping to hide the evidence from the public, they weighed down the dead whales with steel chains and anchors, but the carcasses later washed ashore. Griffin ultimately admitted responsibility, and the episode sparked increased interest in regulating the capture of the creatures.

As Sea World monitored the mood of legislators and took increasing heat from animal rights activists, it suffered a setback closer to home. In hindsight, it is remarkable that Shamu, who was trained by people who had never been in the water with an orca, performed for so many years without serious incident, even as her repertoire came to include daring stunts like leaping skyward to launch trainers from her rostrum. By 1971, Sea World's humans were trusting enough of the animal to plan a publicity stunt: news crews would film Shamu giving a bikini-clad woman a ride around her pen. A 19-year-old Sea World secretary, Annette Eckis, agreed to participate.

With TV cameras rolling, Shamu bucked the young woman into the water, seized her leg and dragged her about the pen as she let out terrified screams. To the horror of onlookers, the orca kept her stubbornly locked in its jaws as poles thrust into the tank by would-be rescuers slipped from her grasp. Eckis was finally dragged from the water, rushed to a hospital, and given hundreds of stitches. A subsequent lawsuit suggested that, while cognizant of the inherent dangers of working with killer whales in captivity, Sea World's head trainer had grown too casual about safety precautions.

"Although warned in general terms that the ride involved dangers and aware that she might fall off, plaintiff was confident of her swimming ability and anxious to do it. She had never heard of whales pushing riders around," the court ruled.

The judge went on to write:

> *Burgess had been responsible for training Shamu ever since Sea World first acquired the animal. He knew Shamu was conditioned to being ridden only by persons wearing wetsuits, and that Shamu had in the past attacked persons who attempted to ride her in an ordinary bathing suit: first a Catalina swimsuit model and then Jim Richards, one of the trainers at Sea World. In addition, Burgess had read training records which showed Shamu had been behaving erratically since early March 1971.*

Sea World suffered another setback that June when Kandu became the first of its killer whales to die. Procuring new orcas would only get more difficult. That July, a survey in Washington state concluded that local waters held fewer killer whales than previously thought, giving momentum to a movement to regulate their capture. Then, on August 29, 1971, Sea World's most famous performer died after 6 years in captivity. Already a multi-million-dollar brand, Shamu's name has been appended to performing whales at Sea World ever since.

The orca deaths redoubled Milt's efforts to study the creatures. He pressed staff to document the circumstances of every cetacean's capture in hopes of learning how to avoid health problems. "Was sufficient padding under the whale when he was laid on deck?" he asked. "Was whale transported on pads and inner tubes or placed in a padded rack? How long was whale out of water? Did it thrash about or hurt itself? Was whale kept covered and wet? Were eyes shielded from the sun? Could exhaust fumes have been breathed during transport?"

Regulatory obstacles would mark 1972. George wanted to build a small stadium on Mission Bay for a show featuring stunt water-skiers, but was delayed by the California Coastal Commission. And Sea World was caught off guard by the introduction and passage of the Marine Mammal Protection Act. The corporation had always been free to display any whale, porpoise, walrus, seal, or otter that it could buy or capture. Now, every marine mammal would require a permit. With three parks to stock, "we were spooked," George stated, though the law deemed displaying animals for the public a legitimate purpose.

"The new law was frustrating and difficult for those who operated before its existence," George said, "but Sea World broke through many of the obstacles by helping the federal bureaucracy codify rules of collecting, design of animal enclosures, and how to initiate successful breeding programs." He added that "by a strange quirk of fate... the marine mammal act was a bonanza for Sea World. Although not its intent, the law helped Sea World to become a monopoly. It made it practically impossible for anyone to initiate competition and forced upon potential competitors costly specifications in design and construction of new facilities. It also put severe restrictions on collecting. By default, Sea World became the only major marine entertainment center that had the know-how, the existing facilities and in-hand capital to subsist and expand under the harsh bureaucratic regulations."

A Management Shakeup

Throughout Milt's tenure at Sea World, he faced questions about the optimal pace of the oceanarium's growth. His instincts were in constant tension with his partner. George fought for constant, aggressive expansion. That approach sometimes paid off, as when the Ohio park quickly became more successful than forecast. At its peak, George's autonomy was significant, for he thwarted Milt's efforts at oversight by acting first and asking permission later, an approach he got away with as long as his gambles were paying off.

Then, in 1969, he persuaded the Board of Directors to partner with the Newhall Land Company on Magic Mountain, a roller-coaster park, and oversaw construction on the site, about an hour north of Los Angeles, with his usual spare-no-expense attitude. Over time, costs exceeded the budget so vastly that Sea World was forced to sell its stake at a $2.3 million loss, easily the company's biggest setback to date. Once the shock wore off, a feeling grew among company leadership that George's team needed to be reined in, and that Sea World ought to stick to its core competency, oceanariums.

In the near term, most everyone still agreed that an Orlando park made good sense. But as construction proceeded the board's scrutiny roiled relations. As George saw it, Sea World had a unique opportunity to open a world-class facility in a crowded market. It would be foolish to scrimp on amenities, he decided from his perch in Florida. In his authorized biography, he dwells on disagreements about Shamu Stadium Orlando, the new park's marquee attraction. He was determined to make the outdoor arena air-conditioned, an expense many in San Diego regarded as frivolous. He postponed a reckoning with the Board of Directors by simply spending what he saw fit and presenting the bill as a fait accompli. When he ran over budget, it was only a matter of time before he drew a furious rebuke. Milt authored the letter:

"Dear George,

With all the concern our company (from board members to employees) has had regarding financial discipline, controls and budgets, your signing an $850,000 construction contract for a program that had not yet received board approval was stupid. The question of economic feasibility is important but secondary to your being so dead wrong in going around the board. Other Sea World officers and department heads can't help but be aware of your flippant attitude. You set a lousy example to follow as regards respect for company policy and adherence to established procedure.

Board approval of substantial commitments is not only an established procedure but there are substantial legal consequences involved. Are you really so dumb and conceited that you don't realize:

1) *You need intelligent input from other people to help avoid mistakes.*
2) *That you have an obligation to conduct yourself in ways that encourage this input rather than discourage it.*

You must really be intimidating your executive committee to get unanimous support from them on such a marginal and questionable expansion. Becker is stuck with the overhead—And such a large expenditure robs him of many future options. How much input did you really get from Becker? The more I think about what's happened here the more concerned I get about overall cost controls and more problems between you and Dave.

Use your head!"

Sea World Orlando opened on December 15, 1973, early enough to iron out any kinks before the summer high season. But cost overruns contributed to a need to arrange new loans and refinance old debts. George still responded to his rebuke with obstinacy. "It is the Board's job to ratify our targets and judge our progress in meeting them and I will facilitate that process," he wrote. "Some members of the board fail to understand that the Board's job is not to manage the parks but this is something we can work out and I welcome the interchange. Don't panic! The Board has sponsored a strong management group."

The Board disagreed.

Under pressure from a majority that had lost trust in his judgment, George resigned as president of Sea World at the January 25, 1974, board meeting. He believed that Milt meant to take over as CEO. In fact, Dave DeMott succeeded him, and Milt resigned his post as Chairman of the Board, taking an at-large seat instead, so that George could have the Chairman title. Despite all that had happened, he hoped his partner would focus on his great talent: developing new attractions.

But George's personality proved too strong for a diminished role. He wrote in a May 30, 1974, letter that after making "a great dream come true" and taking "an idea to preeminence," the Board "relieved me of my duties and conferred the title of Chairman of the Board, along with a sizable salary and other benefits," asking "little of my efforts, time or ideas" in return. "I have too much pride and enthusiasm, and too many ideas to remain in this inactive status," he wrote. "I have concluded that the only honorable course of action… is to resign as Chairman of the Board, effective immediately."

George would make a fleeting attempt to seize control of the company with outside investors, but his machinations failed, and he would never again factor in the oceanarium he co-founded. He went on to found Wet 'n Wild, a successful chain of water parks. At the end of that impressive second act, an industry group named him "Father of the Water Park." He died of lung cancer in 2006, survived by a wife and four children.

Fending Off a Hostile Takeover

With new financing and a tighter hold on the purse strings, Milt was cautiously optimistic about Sea World's prospects. "For the first time in our history, internally generated funds are at a level which allows us to make significant capital improvements at our existing parks," he reported to shareholders in 1975, "enabling us to keep our parks competitive and growing, servicing our debt, and still have additional funds for investment." SeaWorld's biggest concern was the emerging world energy crisis. "Even if no relief were to develop this year and even if our overall attendance were to drop significantly, we are now financially prepared," Dave reassured stockholders. "There is great uncertainty as to what the effect will be of curtailment of pleasure automobile driving due to the gasoline shortage. The San Diego and Ohio parks may actually benefit because of people seeking wholesome entertainment closer to home. Conversely, there is also good reason to believe Sea World of Florida may suffer if the crisis persists, since success in that market appears to be more dependent upon a large influx of motoring tourists."

As it turned out, attendance grew even in Orlando. In fact, that park's earnings exceeded $1 million for the first time. SeaWorld's success that year suggested that it was undervalued. Assessing its stock, Milt began to worry about a hostile takeover. To prepare, he filed away form letters to send investors in case anyone attempted to buy up a controlling share. By October 1976, entertainment giant MCA had purchased 8 per cent of Sea World. Its leaders explicitly assured Milt that they weren't seeking a controlling interest. But before the month was out MCA had written Sea World stockholders with a $22-per-share offer for unlimited shares.

Milt was determined to quash the bid, and not just because he was angry about being misled. MCA's Universal Pictures had just released Jaws in 1975. Its sensationalistic portrayal of sharks rankled Sea World hands, who saw it as anathema to the park's culture. "Sea World is in business not only to make profits, but to create a new movement in our country; a movement committed to the preservation and protection of marine life–and one of the world's most precious vital resources," Milt wrote in a letter opposing the takeover. "What the public sees at Sea World is just the tip of the iceberg. From the date our company was founded, our staff has been engaged not only in entertainment-related activities, but in extensive research and educational projects. We have not only performed an important public service function, but have increased the potential for future growth in our business."

Insofar as MCA undervalued that project, it undervalued Sea World, he asserted, telling shareholders that "Sea World is worth far more than its current market price," and that absorption into MCA "would seriously impede the realization of our corporate goals." He defined those goals in terms of that same cycle he took to be core to the company, giving it "an historic and ever-expanding opportunity to grow." To be long on Sea World, he argued, was to be long on the sea. "Our successes are tied closely to the public's expanding interest and continually increasing curiosity in the marine environment and the creatures found there," he wrote. "Sea World's marine theme is one that few businesses have and one which can only benefit from the exploding world-wide interest in the seas. Investment in Sea World is a means by which you can participate in the public's ever-growing fascination."

He concluded with an appeal to corporate responsibility at a time when the notion was not yet expected. "We would not want you to misinterpret what we are saying. Our primary function is to encourage people to visit our parks," he declared. "Our other activities, however, are almost as important. They reflect recognition that there is a new business ethic demanded from our corporate society, an ethic which requires that a company do more than simply generate profits… adhering to this ethic in the past convinces us that Sea World's unique blend of corporate goals will allow our company to prosper."

Management would have preferred to go on as before, but it soon became clear that Sea World would need to find another suitor if it hoped to stave off MCA. Milt and others felt drawn to the textbook publisher Harcourt Brace Jovanovich, believing its educational mission dovetailed nicely with Sea World's vision for its oceanariums. A courting process began, and HBJ made it clear that they would plan to keep existing management in place if a deal could be struck. *The San Diego Evening Tribune* announced the consummation of the new relationship in a banner headline on November 6, 1976.

NEW SEA WORLD BID: $45 MILLION OFFERED

Investors were paid $28.75 per share, a huge profit for most of them. By year's end, the deal went through. The textbook publisher owned Sea World. Milt would continue to preside over the board, oversee its finances, and advance the oceanarium's interests, but would never again exert the same influence on its future.

Nine

The Evolution of a Conservationist

Killer whales remain Sea World's most iconic, most popular, and most controversial attraction. Large crowds gather daily in stadiums built around orca habitats, where they delight in watching the creatures leap and dive, even as animal rights activists press longstanding objections to putting orcas on display. The anti-captivity position made gains in the court of public opinion after the 1993 Warner Brothers film *Free Willy* and the 2013 documentary *Blackfish*, which chronicles the life of Tilikum, a male orca who killed Sea World trainer Dawn Brancheau. Her 2010 death marked the end of Sea World killer whale shows where trainers performed in the water. The company has since announced that it will phase out its breeding program and end theatrical orca performances by 2017 in San Diego and 2019 at its other marine parks. Its existing whales will remain on display in artificial habitats.

For Milt, who retired in 1985, putting trainers in orca shows was sufficiently uncontroversial that he never addressed the matter (save for choosing to ride an orca himself). But he did respond to critics who questioned whether Sea World ought to capture and display killer whales at all. His most formal answer was delivered on April 30, 1976, when a Senate committee held hearings prompted by early orca roundups. Many were upset at the treatment of Pacific Northwest orcas and the fact that more were killed than captured. Some sought to ban taking any more orcas from the wild.

Milt argued that capturing and displaying orcas was the right thing to do for their species and ours. Abroad, he told Congress, "1,500 killer whales are slaughtered annually for industrial purposes or human consumption." America, however, was on a different trajectory. "Why has there been such a change in attitude toward killer whales in just the last 12 years?" he asked legislators. "Prior to that time," he said, "they were feared, shot at and destroyed as unwanted predators, and even killer whales collected within this period have exhibited bullet holes. By providing an environment for people to come into close contact with these animals to observe, enjoy and learn about them, oceanariums have endeavored to promote a greater understanding and appreciation of marine animals and their environment, engendering in the public a real concern and empathy for them." He insisted that "the tremendous change in attitude of the United States is directly attributed to the effectiveness of the oceanariums."

Going forward, "broad support for conserving killer whales and their habitat would not long endure" if future generations no longer had close contact with the creatures, he warned. In contrast to an animal rights group like PETA, which holds that "animals are not ours to eat, wear, experiment on, or use for entertainment," Milt believed that the lost freedom of a small number of orcas was justified by the utilitarian benefits that they conferred on the rest of their kind, the crowds of happy humans that enjoyed them, and the ocean.

"We will have 5.5 million people through Sea World this year who will learn about the killer whales through seeing the animals," he testified. "Killer whales have been the focal point of interest for the more than 25 million Americans who have visited Sea World," he added, and to eliminate them "would not only deprive the majority of Americans their only opportunity of experiencing these unique creatures, but it would also curtail valuable programs of education and research."

To many with no opportunity to engage with the marine environment, "oceanariums *are* the sea," he declared, concluding that the few orcas taken "are an insignificant number when compared to the benefits they provide to their species."

A Conservationist Gets His Start

Milt's attitude towards marine creatures was shaped by the Christian stewardship that his parents taught, the hard-headed utilitarianism that he absorbed
during the war, his generation's faith in advancement through science, and the
years that he spent observing the ocean. Yet his actions were driven as pow-
erfully by his conviction that whatever their backgrounds and world views,
recreational fishing enthusiasts, people who drew their living from the ocean,
and those who sought to conserve its creatures could and should cooperate as
stewards of the sea. His life would repeatedly test whether those pursuits were
as harmoniously aligned as he wanted to believe.

They converged as never before in 1963. Having drawn on his reputation
as an angler to attract investors in Sea World, Milt approached his colleagues
on its Board with a request: he wanted to found a not-for-profit research institution, legally independent of the marine park but closely associated with it.
Sea World should set aside a small part of its capital to fund the non-profit, he
declared, arguing that the oceanarium had a unique opportunity to advance
marine science and that a nonprofit would lend credibility to the enterprise.
He saved what he thought of as his strongest argument for last: it was the right
thing to do. Sea World would profit from creatures owned by all humankind,
he noted, even if legally speaking, they belonged to no one. Thus, the company should return to the sea a measure of what it took.

His colleagues disagreed unanimously. Corporate social responsibility
wasn't yet a pervasive notion in American life and the board doubted the pre-
diction that the public would hold them to any altruistic standard. Jeff Ascher
recalls expressing the majority sentiment. "I felt that it wasn't appropriate,"
he recalled. "Sea World was a moneymaking operation. And at that time, it
wasn't even clear that there would be any profits for our investors, who were
risking their money on the business. Why would we use some of our funds for
research on fishes, even if it was something that Miltie loved?"

Milt's resolve was rooted partly in his more general belief that one should
give back to the world more than one takes. His parents had instilled a literal approach to meeting that standard: they deliberately conceived and raised
three children so that husband and wife would add one more life to creation

than they lived. Now raising three children of his own, Milt began to approach stewardship of the ocean with the same exacting mindset. Over the course of his life, he wanted to account for literally every fish that he had caught— a daunting ledger. Beyond his youthful hauls at Santa Monica and marlin that he caught as well as anyone on the West Coast, Milt had spent countless hours in the prior decade angling for white seabass and halibut off the coast of Orange County. And he had taken numerous long-range trips to catch tuna.

Chuckie Gardener bore witness to the myriad fish that Milt had pulled from the sea. At 9 or 10, Chuckie got his start as a deckhand on Milt's first boat and retired as captain of his last boat. He would spend more oceango-ing days with Milt than anyone, and recalled deep-water tuna fishing as the most intense. Milt and his fellow fisherman would stand side-by-side at the rail, salt-spray stinging their eyes. They held sturdy but flexible jackpoles, the butt ends anchored by a socket in heavy-duty belts encircling their waists. As the boat crested on swells they rose in the air. In troughs their knees might dip into the ocean. They slapped at the water with jackpoles, wire leaders, and four-inch hooks of shiny, galvanized steel, then braced as muscular fish torpedoed to the surface, attacking the shiny hooks. Marshaling arm muscles and the flex in their poles, they heaved tuna out of the water and up over their shoulders.

All the while, Milt would bark out instructions to avoid a man slipping overboard on decks slick with fish slime or getting cracked in the skull by a hook while standing in the wrong place.

Chuckie remembered the scenes well:

He'd have friends come, but a lot of them only came once. They thought that they'd be out sipping cocktails, sunning themselves, and doing some leisurely fishing. But no. You were on detail. He would be barking out orders. He knew exactly what to do, and he didn't hesitate to tell you how to stand, where to move, when to get out of the way. He acted like he was leading everyone into battle, like the stakes were that high.

We used to call him Commander Shedd. He couldn't be that person in a boardroom or his living room. But the ocean was a different world.

Intense moments could be had and people challenged and led: 'You're not doing it right; you let that fish get away you clumsy so and so.' He wasn't trying to disrespect anyone. It's just that he was the man in charge and he acted like it. He enjoyed being surrounded by people he liked, but he was there to catch fish. If you were too, you'd love it. You'd catch more fish than you ever imagined.

Knowing that commercial fleets took orders of magnitude more fish than even the most successful recreational outings, Milt began to see that careful study would be vital to monitoring fish stocks and innovating to conserve them.

Before pitching Sea World's board on a non-profit, he consulted with leading marine biologists, who confirmed his impression that marine research was woefully underfunded. "The progress man has made exploring and understanding the seas is of practically no consequence when measured against the total to be accomplished," he once declared, likening the efforts to date to a Martian investigating earth from a space ship, "suspended at 30,000 feet, at night, above cloud cover, through which he drops grappling hooks and butterfly nets suspended on thousands of feet of cable to snag evidence."

With access to Sea World facilities and marine animals, researchers could achieve breakthroughs on topics as diverse as ocean life itself, Milt thought. Each animal could benefit the business, its patrons, and marine scientists. Convinced that this was the best way to fulfill his personal debt to the ocean and Sea World's corporate obligations, he pressed his colleagues, answering their arguments and refusing to let the matter drop. "To a man, everyone started out against him," Ascher recalled. "In hindsight, we didn't have a chance," he marveled. "Milt was just too dominant a character. There were small modifications to his proposal, so that Sea World got a little something out of it. But I probably would've given in anyway. George and Davey also decided to placate Milt. He wasn't asking for that much money. And he wanted it so damned much."

The Hubbs-Sea World Research Institute was born. Now named in honor of Carl Hubbs, the renowned ichthyologist, the fledgling nonprofit was still called The Mission Bay Research Foundation in 1963. It remains unusual among corporate-affiliated nonprofits in commencing operations before its main underwriter. That August, Congressman Bob Wilson noted that a new nonprofit in his district "could well turn San Diego into the leading oceanographic research center in the United States." It was "developed with private capital as a nonprofit venture in connection with Sea World," he explained to colleagues who were hearing about the planned oceanarium for the first time. The attention gave Milt credibility when he approached San Diego that fall seeking land for its headquarters. The city granted 15 acres adjacent to the marine park.

From then on Milt would lead the nonprofit in addition to his duties to Sea World, his investment clients, and his family. Its early work was supported not by administrative staff in San Diego, but by Peggie, who did the books on her kitchen table. Milt would continue to preside over the nonprofit's board of directors even after retiring from Sea World, and gave money to ensure its survival until his death. But in 1963, his most pressing task was organizing a demonstration project to justify the foundation's tax-exempt status.

With the help of Frank Mather of the Wood's Hole Oceanographic Institution, he developed one of the West Coast's earliest scientifically controlled tagging programs. Wildlife officials had long wanted better information on migratory fishes. But the cost of chartering vessels to tag them seemed prohibitive. Milt thought that he saw a way to tag more fish for less money than anyone thought possible. Why should the state charter boats at great expense? He knew plenty of recreational fishermen with boats. He knew skippers and men on commercial fishing boats too. Many were friends of his, or at least friendly acquaintances. And wouldn't they be as curious as he was about how many tunas were in local waters, how far they traveled, and how best to conserve them? If recreational and commercial fishermen would allow tagging crews to ride along on their vessels and be alert for tags in future hauls, the expense of the operation would fall so dramatically that it would be viable. Would Fish and Game let the fledgling nonprofit coordinate a tagging expedition?

At first, the official in charge doubted that area fishermen would help. Milt granted that "skepticism regarding a tagging task force is certainly justified," but argued that his plan would work thanks to help that a friend of his could offer. Elmer Hehr was a fellow sportfisherman who owned a 90-foot vessel and had a knack for knowing where the fish were, so much so that recreational and commercial fisherman alike would radio him to ask advice. An early supporter of the Mission Bay Research Foundation, he agreed to draw on his contacts to help its first project to succeed. "Mr. Hehr has put enough of these skippers on good schools of fish to have gained something of a reputation with them," Milt explained to Fish and Game officials, adding that, having already surveyed the local commercial fleet, he found them more cooperative "than even I had hoped for" due to their mutual friend's involvement.

He suggested that Mr. Hehr rendezvous with Fish and Game's tagging expert, Mr. Clemens, for an experimental day of tagging. In the event of failure, "we'll take another approach," he wrote.

The day's success was a portent of Milt's future role in conservation. Its most noteworthy feature wasn't the number of fish tagged, though there were many, but the diverse interests that aligned to make it happen in a manner more efficient than any could have achieved alone. Profit-seeking Sea World and its entrepreneur Chairman of the Board played a role through a nonprofit organization. A government agency was a core player. Its staffers were aided by a wealthy sport-fisherman and yacht owner, as well as sport and commercial fishermen. The tagging data would be useful to scientists, resource managers, even commercial fleets and sport-fishermen. There weren't many people with the foresight and ability to bring people from all those worlds into cooperation.

And afterward, true to character, Milt gave others all the credit. Every nonprofit must keep its backers sold on the value of its projects, he wrote. "I want to thank Mr. Clemens and Mr. Craig for presenting such a clear, complete picture to Mr. Hehr of your fisheries research." His letter slyly proceeded to enlist Fish and Game's director as a future ally in touting the value of the Mission Bay Research Foundation. "The help which Mr. Hehr is extending to our Foundation and to the research activities of your department can be expanded beyond those projects you and I have discussed to date," he wrote. "All that will be required of us, I'm sure, is to substantiate to his satisfaction the need and importance of the programs to be undertaken. There are many demands on his time, talents, and money, hence we must be as thorough and convincing as possible."

That August, Mr. Clemens sent Milt a friendly note on Fish and Game letterhead. Its ostensible aim was to tell him about a one-pound fish caught and tagged aboard Mr. Hehr's vessel. Twenty days later, it had been recaptured and turned in by a commercial fisherman. The approach that Milt had urged was working, Clemens wrote, "providing necessary data concerning albacore movements." He added, "we plan to discover what events order the start of a trans-Pacific migration." Only then did the state official come to his true purpose. "The next step should include a substantial series of aquaria experiments," he wrote. "Our limited resources will not permit funding such experiments, but the new information which may result would be of great scientific value. Therefore, I would like to suggest you consider having the Mission Bay Research Foundation support us in this worthwhile endeavor."

A symbiotic relationship had been fostered. Fish and Game had new resources to draw on. Milt could justify not-for-profit status to the IRS. And he could cite a success when hitting up donors. As he noted in a letter to his friend Herb Bell, the collaboration tagged nearly 700 albacores and bluefin and led directly to a joint study of albacore migratory habits. "With the reputation that we've already established… all we need to be on our way is a little additional financial help to build our working capital," Milt wrote. "Please help us, Herb—I'm sure that in a relatively short time you will be proud you did."

Herb wasn't alone. Milt built up a small base of loyal donors who would support the non-profit over many years as it leveraged its proximity to Sea World's creatures and facilities, sought and won government grants, and undertook original research. But before Sea World had opened its gates or filled its displays, Milt decided that the nonprofit could best contribute to marine research in the short term by playing a coordinating role. It would locate, catalog, and arrange scholarly literature produced on the marine environment for the use of anyone engaged in the field. The effort would include "a library service that supplies subscribers with copies of articles in any of 400 scientific journals cited in the index," the *San Diego Union* reported. The index was mailed monthly to subscribers, including the U.S. Naval Oceanographic Office, the California Department of Fish and Game, Washington State Library and the Scripps Institute. Requests for articles would typically be answered the following business day.

By the late 1960s, a U.S. Fish and Wildlife Service office noted that "this is our first source of referral." UC Research Library called it "heavily used" and "one of the most outstanding specialized indexes available." The Bureau of Commercial Fisheries, Florida, said it is "probably our most valuable reference tool." Chevron Oil Field Research Corporation declared it "a very useful tool in petroleum exploration and producing research." Said a Department of the Navy Director, "It is always a pleasure to write and congratulate one on a job exceedingly well done." And the US Department of the Interior's Pascagoula, Mississippi, office declared it "a valuable addition to any library." Advances in communication technology would ultimately render the coordinate index obsolete. But by then, the Mission Bay Research Institute had a world class collection of marine creatures next door to its facilities and plenty of grants, staff-driven scholarship, and commissioned research projects.

Throwing the Harpoon

Swordfish are "the noblest of all sea fishes," Zane Gray declared after one of his legendary adventures. The predatory species shows great bursts of speed in pursuit of prey and reaches 10 feet or more in length from tail-fin to the tip of their sword-like bill. "To go to work on a broadbill meant a great deal," he wrote. "It meant to lift and haul and pump with the rod, to lower the tip swiftly and wind the reel desperately, and to repeat that performance endlessly." To pursue that same quarry, Milt preferred the method used by Native American fishermen before the arrival of the Spanish: a harpoon held aloft in an upraised arm and thrown down at his quarry. If tuna fishing reminded him of chaotic combat on the line, swordfishing was more akin to the jungle patrols that he had led, with a team collaborating to locate a target, to sneak as close as possible, and to strike at the most opportune moment.

Milt taught himself the method in the early 1960s with his youngest son. Before going after fish they practiced throwing the harpoon at pieces of trash, kelp, any little thing they came across. "Finally it's time for the real thing," Bill said. "Picture a pole-vaulting pole with a lily iron and a dart on the end. The pole itself has flex. You're standing on the end of a 25-foot plank, trying to harpoon a moving fish. And the boat isn't just bobbing up and down, it's swaying side-to-side too. It's not an easy thing to do."

The whole process suited Milt. First, it was necessary to spot a swordfish as its dorsal and tail fins breached the surface—something that could take hours of scanning the ocean. When a harpoon boat finally draws near a swordfish, adrenaline courses through everyone on board. The harpooner, a role Milt nearly always assumed, makes his way to the end of a long plank extending from the bow, so he is perched directly above the water, looking intently for the creature. When it is spotted up close, instructions are shouted to the bridge, where the captain positions the boat in the best possible place. To that point, Milt felt like a commanding officer coordinating a raid. Then the presence of his team would fade.

Alone at the end of the plank, the boat pitching up and down and swaying, Milt would focus on the swordfish, a dancing shadow in the water. Harpoon cocked in his right arm, he threw at the opportune moment, aiming for ten square inches just behind the dorsal fin. When his aim was true, a bronze dart pierced the flesh. As it stuck, the shaft fell away and a rope line tied to the dart unspooled as the startled swordfish swam off. The line was tied at the other end to a buoy or "float" that bobbed at the surface as the swordfish struggled against it. The float was left on the water, marked by a flag, as the swordfish tired.

The search for the next quarry would commence immediately. Thanks to eyesight that was already legendary among Southern California marlin sportfishermen, Milt spotted finning swordfish, using binoculars or the naked eye, uncommonly well. He often directed a captain to an area of ocean two miles off, having gotten a brief glimpse of twin fins that were all but invisible to skeptical companions. He reveled in being able to spot them better than anyone else. And the hours of searching, high up in the crow's nest with bin-oculars scanning the seascape, was an ocean-lover's delight.

Looking all over for game fish, he saw countless porpoises, seals, and whales. Once introduced to these larger mammals, "you start to pick the most exotic, the most exciting, the ones with the best stories to think about," he once reflected. "When they're not too well known and you have access to these animals, you become more involved. The story of my life and marine mam-mals hinged on my involvement with killer whales. I trace my story to being out looking for marlin or swordfish or tuna, and then running into killer whales and seeing their extraordinary involvement with their environment."

Once, he came upon fifteen or twenty killer whales making a commotion. They'd somehow gotten ahold of three ten-foot sharks, which they had killed. And they were playing with their carcasses. He used a tape recorder to describe the scene in detail:

A killer whale would grab a shark, wrest it away from the mouth of another, and take off for 50 or 100 yards. The killer whale possessing the shark treated it like a child would treat a toy. He didn't want to be imped-ed in any way with his happy fun time. He would speed off to what he felt was a safe area and throw the shark as high and far as he could. The other killer whale acted like he had been mistreated. So he would grab the shark away and race back to the central location. Then I noticed that, off on the side, there were two other pairs going through the same routine with two other dead sharks. I was impressed with how these sharks were not eaten.

He delighted in sharing his reconnaissance:

When I got back to my fishermen friends, I would tell them about these killer whales that had obviously captured sharks for this game. They thought that this was ridiculous, that killer whales were interested only in food, that they wouldn't have the sense for organized play. Later, when we had the killer whales on display at Sea World, all the training involved getting them to repeat playful movements they made in the wild. There was nothing strange about their jumping, or anything fundamentally new that they were taught. It was behavior they'd do naturally, though not all the time. We would attach a signal to show that we appreciated a behavior and wanted it done on command. They were delighted to cooperate, even teasing us with antics that could be brought into structured use.

Milt's most memorable experience with wild orcas came much later, during a Hubbs expedition to tag swordfish. A spotter plane was aloft to help spot the creatures, and the pilot excitedly radioed Milt to bring the boat to where he was circling. As Milt drew near, he was amazed to see 28 killer whales attacking a 60-foot blue whale, which was swimming due north. "The killer whales had a regular military formation: they had one or two scouts out front; there were six or seven killer whales always grabbing onto the tail of the blue whale; and there were another six or eight killer whales ripping and tearing on the back of the blue whale," he recounted. "Two more were on the flank, as if to ward off other predators. And behind this moving mass were four baby orcas and one big bull."

The bull kept the babies out of harm's way as the blue whale struck out with his tail. The killer whales were doing more and more feeding, tearing off chunks of blubber and muscle. "We would be startled to see, when the light was right, one of the animals come up near the surface with a substantial piece of flesh hanging out of its mouth," he said. "One animal had a 25-pound piece of flesh that extended off the left side of his jaw a foot or more. I watched, fascinated, while he manipulated the meat with his jaws so as to swallow it without its washing away because of the force of the moving water."

He marveled at his good luck

The sea was glassy calm and the light just right, so you could occasionally see under the water to orcas pressing to the side of the blue whale, vibrating the way a shark vibrates to make his teeth dig in and cut. The baby whales were kept out of harms way until the blue whale was swimming a knot or two knots only. Then the big whales backed off and allowed the babies to move in. A cameraman who happened to be on board captured over an hour of the attack. What we were looking at was a presentation of what occurred naturally in the ocean. To me, the killer whales were intelligently teaching their young how to attack a blue whale: keep out of harm's way until they're softened up enough that they could eat it. We saw the magnificent yet horrendous cruelty of life as it really existed.

Milt had affection for Sea World's captive orcas, who sometimes reminded him of Phantom X, his boyhood dog, in the way that they would greet their favorite trainers. But he never forgot that they were the same apex predators who brutally dominated sharks, seals, fish, and other whales. It struck him as equally natural for man to dominate orcas, even as he felt humans had an obligation to conserve the species and its habitat.

At Sea World, he was more interested in seeing orcas play in ways that hinted at their natural behavior than watching scripted shows. But he knew fewer patrons would bond with the creatures without anthropomorphized antics. Watching a 6-year-old exit a Sea World gift shop hugging a Shamu stuffed animal to her chest, he once again perceived a harmonious alignment of his goals. Through the oceanarium, a child had come to have affection for orcas that might last a lifetime. On return visits, she would spend money that would help Milt to serve investors and provide for his progeny. And as long as Sea World endured, its animals and a portion of its profits would assist Hubbs in the study and conservation of the marine environment, benefitting fishermen, hungry humans, and future generations.

He felt indignant at the notion of Sea World being denied the orcas it needed to thrive. "It is a paradox," he insisted to Congress during his 1976 testimony, "that organizations such as oceanariums, which have themselves been responsible for creating much needed awareness and respect for such animals... have become the target." Without them, he worried, the masses would lapse back into ambivalence about their fate. "Animals need a concerned, interested, informed public for their survival," he told legislators. "People become interested and involved only when they have had personal contact. Nearly everyone who ever sees a killer whale will do so in oceanariums."

Conservation and the Cold War

Milt would see the concerns and challenges of every era through the lens of the ocean. After Sputnik, as America's attention turned to outer space, he had assured anyone who would listen that the underwater world would be more important to besting the Soviet Union. Efforts to map the sea bottom and state-of-the-art acoustics would stop Russian subs from sneak attacks. Energy extracted from the sea floor would confer advantages. And just as space research was easiest to sell as a defense priority, so too was funding for oceans.

"To most of us," he told a San Diego audience, "the sea has meant, primarily, recreation and pleasure." But lately, he continued, "the pleasant connotations I've enjoyed have been giving way more and more to a sense of concern, even alarm."

He cited three reasons for his concern:

1) *our nation is locked in a life and death struggle with the communists;*
2) *effective utilization of the marine environment and its resources will play a far more important role in the long term outcome of this struggle than our nation yet realizes;*
3) *the Russians are more aware of the importance of the ocean environment and more dedicated to its mastery than are we.*

Most any oceanic fact could be seen through the lens of national defense. "The porpoise is thought to exceed the hydrodynamic efficiency of our best ships," Milt told Hubbs donors. "If man could duplicate the feat, the savings of energy would be worth many millions." Another time he mused that "where once it would have seemed only an interesting fact that a certain, strange little sea snail is able to manufacture teeth whose structure is almost one-half pure manganese, I now wonder if we are doing enough to study this animal."

Once, while trying to capture a pilot whale to display at Sea World, Milt slipped a net over the head of a 7-foot baby. He recounted what happened next in a speech about how marine biology could assist the military. They had hoped to use the baby whale to capture its mother. "She was much too smart and stayed maybe a foot to two feet out of our reach," he said. "During this period, 20 whales that had initially been with mother and baby moved away from our boat about two to three miles and were meandering all over the ocean. As amazing as it may seem, the mother and baby always swam in a perfectly straight line towards where the pod of whales were located, giving conclusive evidence that they were in constant contact with these whales although they were almost out of sight. The Navy has more than just an academic interest in the fantastical acoustical accomplishments of these creatures."

By the mid 1970s, Cold War fears receded, and advances in tagging afforded new opportunities to learn about West Coast fishes like albacore, marlin, and blue fin tuna. The new data stoked Milt's belief that conservation of fish stocks was a more urgent priority than he had previously realized—that, contrary to what many believed, the ocean was not inexhaustible even in their lifetime. "He thought one of the most sobering aspects of the blue fin tagging program was the fact that of one group of 100 blue fin tuna tagged and released from a purse seiner's net, there were 39 recoveries made in three years, showing how vulnerable the blue fin could be to modern fishing technology," Bill said. "He took this as an indication that certain species could be at far greater risk than what was generally acknowledged, that there was much that needed to be learned about pelagic fish, and that it could be learned."

If Milt worried more than the average American about fish stocks, however, he worried even more about a problem that seemed like it would manifest sooner: as global population exploded, would there be enough food? He believed that if science, business and fishermen cooperated, a coming shortage could be averted, but was dismayed that inquiries into how to increase and more efficiently harvest the sea's protein—goals many saw in tension with one another— had scarcely begun. Where, for example, were the inquiries into aquaculture?

"Man has used certain very visible resources from the sea with an attitude that they existed in unlimited quantity," Milt observed in the summer of 1976. "He's exploited these visible and easily accessible assets with little thought to the cause and effect relation of what impact he was having—and, of course, he's used the seas as a vast garbage dump, for recreation purposes and for a means of transportation. It's only been very recently that he's looked at the sea with a truly serious attitude."

In 1977, Mission Bay Research Foundation was rededicated. It would henceforth be known as Hubbs-Sea World Research Institute. Though still legally separate, the non-profit and the oceanarium would cooperate even more closely. Both entities gained from highlighting their relationship. The non-profit enjoyed the prestige of a global brand, increased visibility for its research, and the implicit commitment of ongoing support. Sea World increased goodwill and enhanced its credibility. Since before selling its first ticket, its assets had been "providing a vital contribution to mankind's research efforts in understanding marine creatures," Milt told Congress, citing a history of more than 30 major research projects. One involved providing the University of Washington with two killer whales, support facilities, veterinary services, boats and personnel. "The purpose," he stated, "is to tag these whales with radio transmitting devices in order to further compile much needed data relative to the population dynamics and migration patterns of killer whales."

Sea World's board no longer doubted the wisdom of the nonprofit. "Milt raised money for the fishes because he loved them," Ascher said, "and in the beginning I never believed it would really help the business. But Milt turned out to be right: times changed and people started expecting more of corporations. They could honestly say that Sea World had invested in the environment from the first, that they learned extremely valuable things about the animals in their shows. Milt was the one who saw the value in that. He made it part of the culture, and he created the conditions for everyone to come around."

After Milt's retirement in 1985, he would no longer exercise influence over the oceanarium's direction, the behavior of its management, or where it would situate itself on the spectrum from aquarium to amusement park. But Sea World continued to support the nonprofit that bore its name, and Milt would remain proud of the business he helped to found and root for its success. He lived out his remaining years believing that, through the interest in the ocean that Sea World stoked and the corporate and personal philanthropy it enabled, the business had helped him return to the sea more than he took.

A New Business for Milt and Peggie

A sportfisherman in pursuit of a marlin must travel to a port, charter a boat, and burn fuel to reach deep water. The cost in dollars alone is high. But for those who have the money, the more precious commodity is time. Even if calm seas hold, daylight and provisions are fixed— and often as not, there are obligations back on land. Since many hours of trolling are typically needed to hook a single marlin, each encounter is a scarce, precious, fleeting opportunity. Success in such moments requires not just skill, luck, and hard work, but preparation to limit anything that could go wrong. That's why most every world-record marlin caught in living memory was reeled in on a sportfishing rod outfitted with something called a roller guide. Affixing that tiny piece of hardware to a rod might add $100 to its cost. Yet it allows the fishing line to run over a tiny wheel rather than a flat surface, reducing friction that could weaken a line and cost a fisherman the catch of a lifetime. It insures against a broken line at a climactic moment.

During the 1950s, Milt, for whom proper planning prevented poor performance, always wanted a roller guide on his rod, though the quality of the hardware on offer in that era was highly variable. Around 1960, he discovered a new roller-guide manufacturer, a company called AFTCO. It was the side-project of engineer and entrepreneur J.C. Axelson, a recreational fisherman who had also been unsatisfied with existing options. Axelson invented his variation in the basement of his Newport Beach home and filed for a patent. A company history describes his efforts as a labor of love more than a business venture. Anglers quickly came to recognize the high quality of his product, so much so that they were scrambling for more roller guides when Axelson died.

Milt learned from his accountant that Axelson's widow was filling orders by running down their inventory; reserves were running low. Would Milt be interested in buying the company?

He knew the product, its reputation among sportfishermen, and the market niche it filled. Its headquarters were minutes from his house. Due diligence confirmed the worth of its intellectual property and machinery. And he liked the idea of owning a company that aimed to solve the problems of sportfishermen. As Sea World's Chairman of the Board, however, he felt that he couldn't ethically purchase AFTCO without bringing news of the opportunity to his fellow board members. In short order, he put together a presentation outlining AFTCO's strengths and weaknesses as a business, the fairness of its asking price, and how Sea World might benefit from acquiring it. His colleagues quickly informed him that, for once, he was thinking with his heart rather than his head. AFTCO did appear to be a good investment, they concurred, but it made no sense for Sea World to sell fishing tackle. If Milt wanted to buy it, he should consider any perceived duty to the company discharged.

He and Peggie quickly arranged the purchase with just one unexpected obstacle: driving home after signing the papers, Milt experienced heart palpitations and drove himself to the nearest hospital. His condition was serious: it required open heart surgery, and he traveled all the way to Houston, Texas, for the operation because so few surgeons were capable of performing it. As Milt convalesced, Peggie had began to do AFTCO's books, a job she would keep for decades, And Milt's brother-in-law, Lawrence Paul, acted as AFTCO's general manager. After recovering, Milt invested in a new headquarters, applied basic business principles to an enterprise that had been a side project, and restarted manufacturing. He also wrote a lot of letters to upset customers who hadn't been able to get delivery of a product that was always in demand. One customer approached at a trade show, demanding, "Are you in the letter-writing business or the roller guide business?" Milt explained the circumstances of the sale and repeated an assurance he made to all his customers: Going forward, there wouldn't be any problems.

Despite Milt's reliance on his wife and brother-in-law to run AFTCO day-to-day, his children never thought of the enterprise as a family business where they would make careers. Their father would always reiterate that they were to make their own way in the world and should never expect to rely on family wealth or nepotism. "He was at arm's length with respect to ability and entrepreneurship," his eldest son recalls. Steve went on to start his own business, drawing on contacts he made while playing baseball in Italy to create and run one of the largest antique furniture operations in California. But when AFTCO needed help on short notice, Milt encouraged his youngest son, who had planned to apply at IBM after college, to seize the opportunity. "There was no 'Welcome to the company, son,'" Bill recalls. "It was, 'If you do a good job it will be worth your while. If you don't, I'm going to fire you.' Now that I'm a dad with kids working here," he added, "I know how much more fun and meaningful that makes it, but as far as I was concerned, this was a job like any other."

Bill was tasked with figuring out how AFTCO could reach new customers. "Dad urged me to have lunch with the head of marketing at Sea World and I learned all of the basics," he said.

Still, Bill felt that no matter how much time he spent at the office, there was always something else he could be doing, some aspect of marketing or the fishing tackle business that he could be studying. "And right from the start, Dad thought that I should be spending a portion of my time on non-profit work," he recalled. "He felt a fishing tackle company had a responsibility to look for ways to do good things for the ocean. And I agreed that giving something back was the right thing to do, but I remember being skeptical that it was the best use of my time when I still had so much to learn. My deference to Dad made it natural for me to start doing the nonprofit work even before I was persuaded that it was the best use of company time at that moment. That was just respect."

Back then, AFTCO counted a few hundred thousand dollars per year in sales and a limited product line of roller guides. Milt went to trade shows, met with foreign customers when they came to visit, reviewed financial statements, ran the board meetings and conducted year-end reviews. But on average, he might spend less than an hour a week at the company.

Still, there was no doubt about who was boss. "We knew he would make the ultimate decision on any issue he wanted to weigh in on," Bill said. "Should there be a price increase? How much? Should we rent or buy that building? Any time we were confronted with big questions, he understood business generally and this business in particular so well that I could spend 5 minutes with him on a complicated matter and he would get it, whereas I could talk to another smart guy about the same subject and after a whole day he still wouldn't understand."

Soon after Bill took a larger role in the business, for example, he was on a sales trip visiting East Coast customers that bought AFTCO roller guides. At that time, fishermen were improving their rods by replacing wooden butts—the thick part of the rod closest to the fisherman's body—with aluminum, which didn't break. "All up and down the coast I saw these aluminum butts," Bill remembers. "But they were all being made in scattered machine shops that couldn't produce them whenever they were busy with their regular orders. Each little pocket of business was insignificant. But if AFTCO could get all that aluminum butt business…"

On a fishing trip with his dad, Bill explained his insight about the possibility of consolidation and the likely returns to scale. But he confessed that he hadn't quite figured out how to carry it off. Milt replied that they should call a friend of his, Jim Easton, who made aluminum bats and knew everything about the business.

"This was a Sunday evening," Bill recalled. "We walked off the boat to a payphone right at the top of the bridge. Dad got him on the phone, explained the situation, and found that Easton was eager to talk. His company had begun to make an aluminum butt with a fishing-rod manufacturer that pulled out of the deal so late that they'd already built some of the tooling." Father and son made an appointment for the next day. "As far as dad's time, he didn't need to do anymore than walk off the boat to a payphone, have a quick conversation, and drive to Van Nuys the next day for a meeting," Bill explained. "But those few hours of his time made possible decades of an aluminum butt business that couldn't have happened without him."

Changing With the Ocean

During the busiest decades of Milt's professional life, while presiding over Sea World, Hubbs, and AFTCO, he still found time for recreational fishing. But most every trip now had multiple purposes. Milt always had his researcher friends as well as his business partners in mind, even when spotting the grandest of quarries. "Bill, you were with me when we tried to catch a live marlin and bring it into Sea World," Milt reminded his son during a session when they traded stories with a tape recorder:

> *We caught this marlin and rigged it with a quarter-inch nylon rope, attaching it to the marlin's bill so there wouldn't be a lot of excess weight. I had to make special knots that wouldn't slip off. We had to tow it roughly 30 miles. A marlin had never been kept in captivity—still hasn't—but we were the first to try, that we know of, and the first to get a marlin on land and in a tank, at least for awhile. The marlin just swam behind us. We thought, he's healthy. But as we got into the greener, dirtier water on the way into Mission Bay, the marlin got more skittish, and near the channel of the harbor it started going crazy and jumping out of the water. Here we had a marlin right at the mouth of Mission Bay, with sailboats all around, other boats going through harbor entrance, and everybody's jaw is dropping! They're watching the marlin jump behind this boat in a place where everybody knows there can't be marlin. Boats started following just to see what was going on. There was quite a commotion!"*

Finally, they got the marlin to Sea World. "The only available holding tank had a bunch of sharks just flown in from the Florida Keys at great expense, so the curator wasn't so excited," Milt said. "We thought they would leave each other alone. They did, at first, but in a skittish moment, the marlin made a fast movement and its bill accidentally hit the side of one of the sharks, penetrating its skin. Just like if you gaff a shark when you're fishing, it started to roll and roll. So the shark dies, the marlin drowns, and the curator says, 'Damn it, Milt, you're not bringing any more marlin into my tanks!'"

Milt had long since changed his attitude toward the creatures. He treated marlin caught in his twenties, thirties, and forties like trophies: along with most sport-fisherman of his generation, he would be photographed standing beside his prize as it was hoisted aloft. Once, he got home in the early morning from an overnight marlin trip and drove his son, Steve, to school with several marlins strapped to his automobile's roof. In his later years, Milt felt chagrin at those once-fond memories. Along with most of the sportfishing community, he began to release his catches back into the sea in an effort to preserve the majestic creature.

His relationship with swordfish was even more complicated. Its evolution over several decades would illustrate both the changes witnessed by fishermen of his generation and the different directions he was pulled by his different passions. Circa 1970, 63 commercial vessels harpooned swordfish in California waters, while a tiny, unknown number of recreational fishermen harpooned for sport. In 1971, however, the California Department of Fish and Game restricted harpooning to commercial vessels with permits. The rule prompted Milt to start a small-scale, commercial harpooning operation, allowing him to comply with the new regulations and to bankroll the expense of doing so.

Five years later, he built his dream vessel, a 67-foot boat christened The Sea World. It was equipped for marine research, facilitating countless Hubbs projects; it had huge tank capacity built into its decks to take on specimens, a business purpose; it afforded Milt the ability to host friends on sportfishing trips; and although every sort of fish would be caught from its deck, it was ideally suited to swordfishing: the fish could be spotted from the crow's nest atop its high mast and harpooned from its 45-foot plank. What's more, the low rear deck and the small live-bait troughs built into the gunnel made it an excellent boat for catching albacore tuna with jackpoles.

Milt poured any profits back into the vessel's upkeep, its crew, and its state of the art equipment. The luxury of fishing to break even rather than to earn a living made him an object of resentment on some competing boats, never more so than when he got a spotter plane. Fishermen had long relied on binoculars to spot swordfish, but beginning in the early 1970s, enterprising sorts began paying pilots to look down at vast swaths of ocean and radio coordinates of swordfish they spotted. Milt quickly adopted the high-capital, high-reward tactic, drawing criticism from those who couldn't afford planes and thought them unfair.

In 1976, California banned spotter planes for a year, due in part to the alarmingly small number of landings. These worries were forgotten in 1978. Old-timers recall it as something like a miracle. Local waters were full of swordfish: nearly 7,000 were taken commercially. Few imagined that they were at an all-time peak. But the contemporaneous use of drift gill nets in the California bight snagged many swordfish and sharks; and in 1980, when drift gill-netters were allowed to sell swordfish, harpooners saw their takes plummet. The huge, free-floating nets caught an incredible number of fish. By 1984, swordfish harpooners were almost unanimous in lobbying for the unrestricted ability to use planes so that they could compete.

Swordfish stocks were also depleted by long-lining, a method originally developed in Japan—imagine a mile or two of rope, kept afloat by buoys, and vertical fish lines with hooks dangling at regular intervals for the entire length. In 1980, Mexico sought to develop its fishing industry by issuing longline permits for cooperative ventures with foreign entrepreneurs. Milt, who'd been fishing Mexican waters for decades and learned of the program before most, secured a permit. "He started a company at Magdalena Bay, about three quarters of the way down the Baja Peninsula," said Chuckie Gardener, the first mate when the venture began. "The idea was to train a Mexican crew so that they'd learn to make use of resources off their coast. They had no idea how to fish like the Japanese did. There hadn't been any incentive to find out, because there wasn't an established market for swordfish in Mexico." In exchange for the government permit, Milt would teach the locals to fish; catch swordfish in their waters; process it using Mexican labor; ferry it north with Mexican truckers; and sell it in America for $5 a pound. "It would help to develop the Mexican economy, so there wasn't so much poverty. Milt invested a lot trying to make it work, but it failed."

That was a blessing in disguise. When Milt got interested in the venture, shortly after the bounty of the 1978 season, the abundance of swordfish was widely assumed. He saw long-lining as an interesting method with which he was curious to experiment and felt it could help address a concern that he had raised in speeches dating back years: the global population was increasing, and poorer countries had to better extract protein from the sea, he felt, or risk famine. Even in 1983, when Mexico cancelled its joint long-lining permits and established a 50-mile sportfishing zone off Baja, Milt's vision seemed viable, even if his particular business hadn't succeeded.

But by 1986, due in large part to drift gillnets, swordfish stocks were in precipitous decline. And just as Milt's attitudes about taking rather than catching and releasing marlin had evolved, so too did he rethink long-lining. In fact, as he better understood the damage longlines caused, he ceased all involvement with the gear. Studies would confirm what he had observed on the ocean: miles of hooks snagged many more swordfish than any harpoon boat took, plus a lot of relatively valueless sharks and turtles that were inadvertently hooked, drowned, and wasted. The more Milt studied the science, the more conclusive the arguments against the method seemed.

Later, in 1988, Bill got a phone call from an alarmed contact at the Department of Fish and Game. He warned that an experimental, longline shark fishery recently established in the state was about to become a permanent fishery. "If that happened, the caller warned that the mako shark nursery off Southern California would be in serious jeopardy," Bill said. The official hoped that the Shedd family would lead a last ditch effort to stop it. In Bill's capacity as AFTCO's president, he decided that opposing the shark fishery should be an official company project, similar to AFTCO's efforts to stop commercial fishermen from using drift gill-nets in local waters. As the company's owner, Milt signed off on his son's decision and personally funded AFTCO's efforts to ban longlines, which were led by Bill and AFTCO sales manager Greg Stotesbury.

The effort marked a change for Milt. At first, he had been reluctant to speak out publicly either for or against the technology. As forward looking a conservationist as he was, he grew up in an era when new fishing methods were cause for excitement and celebration. He still believed that efficiently drawing protein from the sea would be indispensable to feeding a growing population. Adjusting to a scarcity of fish more severe than anything he had previously anticipated took time. In this uncharacteristic period of uncertainty, he continued to treat science as his lodestar, and it would ultimately transform many of his views. But as long as he still felt conflicted about a commercial fishing method, he felt it would be unfair to criticize friends who ran affected operations. Their ability to make a living, their mortgages, and the well being of their families were at stake, whereas he had the luxury of catch-and-release fishing as a pastime and personal wealth that permitted him to stop worrying about a paycheck.

For all his life, he had regarded his various pursuits as harmonious: to succeed as a stockbroker, he fished with clients; founding Sea World, he insisted that a non-profit be affiliated with it, mixing business and philanthropy. His dream boat served purposes as varied as tagging fish for science, collecting them for display, and pursuing them for pleasure. Commercial fishing had once seemed to fit so harmoniously into Milt's world. Had he been a man of his father's generation, when fish stocks seemed inexhaustible and fishing methods were less efficient, he could have remained a full-fledged commercial fisherman, a sport-fisherman in good standing, and a conservationist, all without apparent conflict.

But by the 1990s, he couldn't escape the tension between modern fishing methods that he had greeted with optimistic curiosity and the conservation of fish stocks, the issue he cared about most in his final years. As commercial fleets, environmental lobbies, sport-fishermen, and various conservationists staked out their respective territories, all invoking science for their side, a man with stakes and personal friendships in all of those worlds inevitably lost some of them.

Jim Macalear was a commercial fishing buddy that Milt kept. The two had known one another since the 1950s, when Macalear sought help setting up a profit-sharing plan at a company he owned. They became fast friends. In the early 1970s, Macalear would drive as Milt harpooned swordfish. He excelled at positioning the boat in just the right spot, which didn't stop Milt from giving him hell if a swordfish escaped. Once, he uncharacteristically turned the boat in a way that caused a harpooned swordfish to tangle the line around the propeller, Milt wordlessly went below deck, reemerged with a swim mask and fins, and said, "You did it, now go untangle him," sending him down with the fish and its razor-sharp sword.

Macalear appreciated Milt's forthrightness and conscientiousness as a stockbroker, and later, his passion for sharing knowledge about the ocean. But the two came to disagree about fishing regulations as Milt's conservationism evolved. "That was always a contentious thing between us, because I represented commercial fishing boats up and down the coast," Macalear said. Milt had done longlining himself, he added, "and then, he turns around and says don't do this stuff."

The old friends never did reach agreement, but Macalear came to understand Milt's perspective. "I represented three or four swordfish boats up north, and I remember going up to Ventura harbor when a couple of them were offloading," he said. "I noticed this truck driver go to his cab with something wrapped in a towel. I didn't know if he was taking a slice off the swordfish or what. 'Well,' he says, 'when the guys get a little swordfish, they keep him for me and I get them mounted.' They'd caught a perfectly formed swordfish that wasn't more than a foot long. I thought, if they keep going like this, there won't be any swordfish. That's where Milt was coming from. He could see what modern equipment would do to the industry. It switched him over."

Harpooning swordfish would remain Milt's favorite kind of fishing. He thrilled in the hunt, knew that it culminated in taking just the single fish you're after, and felt confident that if scientists continued to study the creatures and policymakers diligently applied their research, a sport-fishery could be sustainably maintained. Indeed, he tried to advance that project directly. "Dad successfully implanted a sonic tag in 5 different broadbill swordfish, an historic first," Bill explained. "One specimen was followed closely for 5 days, developing new insight into the behavioral characteristics of these creatures. The sonic tags provided amazing temperature and depth data. In less than two minutes, a swordfish could transition from 50-degree water at 900 feet to surface water of 80 degrees."

A New Direction for AFTCO

By the mid-1980s, AFTCO had strung together a collection of specialized products that didn't interest bigger companies. Within those niches they dominated, so the question became how to grow the business when they already had such high market share. They didn't want to sell rods and reels—that would put them in competition with their best customers, who bought the bulk of their roller guides, butts, and handles.

One day, Bill was driving to a father-daughter weekend retreat at Forrest Home, a Christian conference center. A friend and his kids were in the car too. The friend was asking how AFTCO could grow. Bill's spur-of-the-moment reply: "We need to make anything and everything that sportfishermen need, right down to the clothes on their back!"

Later that night he began to reflect on the answer he had given. "I thought, 'God, I've never had this idea about the clothing business before, so if we try it and it works, it's coming from you,'" he recounted. "I prayed about it for most of the night and the next morning I was convinced that it was something AFTCO should do." Due diligence confirmed his instinct, so he presented the idea to his father. Milt saw that his son believed strongly in the proposal and gave his blessing with one condition. "I don't care if you fail in the clothing business," he said. "Just don't do anything that will make us fail in the hardware business. If you make bad stuff, it may be cheaper. It may even turn a profit in the short run. But it will hurt the brand and people will not be as likely to buy our hardware. Above all else make sure you make quality clothing."

Neither Milt nor his son were natural clothiers. Their mothers and later their wives had bought most every item in their closets. But the hours that Milt spent on the ocean helped AFTCO on its original fishing short, one of their best-selling products. "Our longtime sales manager, Greg Stotesbury, deserves credit for thinking of a special pocket for fisherman's pliers," Bill said. "But the main thing is that they're bulletproof."

In creating them, Bill had narrowed the choices to three fabrics. Then his dad called on a weekend afternoon, having returned to port with 1,500 pounds of fish. He wanted help cleaning them, so they met in the AFTCO parking lot, where Bill pulled out plastic tables for the chore. "They were going to be a mess of blood and fish guts," Bill said, "so I ran in the office, got those swatches of material, and threw them on the tables."

They absorbed fish guts and blood for hours. For good measure, Bill left the swatches out in the sun to dry out. "By the time I got them home," he remembers, "they couldn't have been filthier." He told his wife that he had to throw them in the washing machine, "and when the cycle was finished I found out what I wanted." The fish blood and guts had washed completely out of just one of the swatches. "If dad had not gone fishing," Bill said, "we never would've thought to do that experiment and we probably would've ended up with a different fabric."

Saving the White Seabass

If Milt's powerful desires to both catch and conserve swordfish had challenged his instinct that all of his pursuits could co-exist harmoniously, his experience with white seabass, another of his frequent quarries, seemed to reaffirm the value of cooperation among the fishing, business, and conservation communities.

Beginning in 1977, Milt helped to underwrite the work of Don Kent, a graduate student researching the growth characteristics of striped bass. Recalling how plentiful the species was in his youth, Milt was alarmed by their scarcity.

In time, concern would be widespread. "Sportfishing catches in California dropped from more than 55,000 fish annually in the early 1950s to fewer than 3,500 in the early 1990s," the *Los Angeles Times* reported in 1995. "Commercial catches dropped accordingly." Don Kent, who gradually rose to lead Hubbs, had already started an experimental program to see whether white seabass whose stocks had declined could be replenished. And in 1990, after years of effort, 2,000 white sea-bass were successfully hatched and released as juveniles into Mission Bay as a proof of concept. All were marked.

The first seabass of legal size was recaptured in March 1992. This success was promising, but a facility that could raise and release white sea-bass on a large enough scale to help sustain the species would cost in excess of $2 million to build. Operating costs would also be significant, and there would be the ongoing challenge of maintaining a diverse brood stock. White sea-bass were rare and skittish, and fishermen would have to go out of their way to keep them alive to turn over for breeding.

Like other observers of the species' decline, Milt wanted to see a hatchery built. He was instrumental in touting the potential benefits of the project, keeping it among the foremost priorities of Hubbs. With his son Bill, AFTCO attorney Mike Duffy, and Don Kent, he sought funding from the California Coastal Commission, which controlled the money that corporations paid to mitigate environmental damage along the coast. The bulk of the funds were secured from two power companies. San Diego Gas and Electric donated land for the hatchery on a lagoon in Carlsbad, California. And Southern California Edison, having previously agreed to mitigate the effects of its nuclear power plant, contributed more than $4 million to the project. Owned by Hubbs, the hatchery would operate under a contract with the California Department of Fish and Game. To this day, it has permission to release 350,000 seabass per year.

Once again, Milt was a driving force behind an effort that would come to fruition only after businessmen, government actors, scientists, and conservationists aligned to support it. The hatchery's success, once operational, would depend on recreational anglers too, as Jim Hendricks later described in *Sportfishing Magazine*. By his calculation, the sportfishing community donates 20,000 hours per year to tending grow-out pens in harbors and inlets. "Young white seabass are transferred from the hatchery to these pens to give the young fish a chance to grow to decent size before release into the ocean," he explained. As well, "anglers assist with the capture and replenishment of the hatchery's brood stock." This cooperation between resource managers and sport-fishermen is a fitting a legacy for Milt, for it is perfectly in keeping with his longstanding philosophy that surprising things can be achieved when people collaborate in good faith for a common purpose. In 2006, four years after Milt's death, Peggie released the hatchery's one-millionth white sea-bass into the ocean.

Ten

Papa Shedd's Legacy

At the turn of the century, Tom Brokaw published a best-selling book on what he dubbed "The Greatest Generation." They were "birth-marked for greatness," he wrote, "from the Great Depression forward, through the war and into the years of rebuilding and unparalleled progress on almost every front." As these men and women began to retire and die, they gave America over to their children, the Baby Boomers, who are now reaching retirement themselves. For Milt's children, who saw their father and mother as twin embodiments of the Greatest Generation, this raised urgent questions. How does a nation with a short attention span conserve the wisdom of elders who accomplished so much as they leave the scene? In eulogizing their triumphs, how do we guard against deifying humans whose flaws and missteps are fruitfully studied? Is it an inspiration or a burden to measure ourselves against their accomplishments?

After grappling with Milt's strengths and flaws in the context of history, his son Steve has reached the conclusion that today's Americans are better at grasping the World War II generation's shortcomings than the benefits of the traditional values and virtues that it espoused. "From his parents, Dad got thrift, an aversion to debt, a strong moral character, discipline, and a tremendous work ethic," Steve said. "And he got respect for authority and fidelity.

Throughout his life, a lot of his motivation was doing his father proud. Before he died, after being in bed for a few days without speaking, he had a burst of energy, and I was there to hear his last words. He said, 'I did everything that my father wanted me to do.'"

For Bill, who tried to make Milt proud in turn, one touchstone, still on display at AFTCO, was Milt's motto: "The most powerful force on earth, other than God," it states, "is two people in trusting cooperation working toward a mutually acceptable goal." In business, "Dad saw that there is a basic conflict between an employer, who wants to create profits, and an employee, who wants to earn as much as possible," he said. "He knew that the only way he could win is to create as big a pie as possible, so you have profit sharing, incentives for workplace safety, and you treat people right. We've always had lesser employee turnover than is found in other companies."

Cooperating with Milt required deference of a sort once expected of children that deviates from today's norms. Even at play, Bill was expected to respect authority and sublimate his ego. When he started swordfishing with his dad, he harpooned the first one he attempted dead on. Two days later, they spotted another. "I nail it, two for two. So I think I'm doing pretty good!" he said. "Another two days go by. Finally, we spot a swordfish and get up alongside it. And I miss."

He still remembers his father's response. "God dammit Billy!" Milt yelled down from the bridge. "We. Don't. Miss! From now on, you're driving, I'm harpooning."

Bill drove the rest of the summer.

"Of course, Dad is obviously not going to get them all that first summer," Bill said. "So when he finally missed, what do you think I said? 'Nice try, Dad.' That was partly the generation, partly his presence and his personality. Turnabout was not fair play. He's the father. I'm the son. You had no opportunity to kid about something like that. You said nothing, or you said, 'Nice try, Dad.'"

His biggest business disagreement with his father was tangential to AFTCO. Each December, Bill would operate a Christmas-tree lot near his house, taking his annual vacation, drawing on contacts from his college days in Oregon, and earning a tidy profit on his own time, or so Bill saw it. But Milt pressed his son to give up the side business. He argued that it deprived AFTCO of a leader who would be recharged after a vacation, and that it would deplete Bill's creative energy. They never did agree on the subject. But Bill ultimately gave in. As on other occasions, the success of the father-son team owed a great deal to the latter's maturity. A competitive man with an ambitious personality, Bill never let ego or an impulse to rebel ruin their ability to cooperate, as has happened in so many businesses where sons joined fathers.

While this required sacrifices, Bill now looks back at some of the times that he deferred and feels grateful. He's glad, for example, that he began dedicating significant time to ocean conservation as soon as he joined AFTCO. The expertise that he gained put him in a position to lobby effectively against the use of gill nets and long lines at moments of need; to push forward the catch-and-release ethic; and to support sportfishing organizations and conservation causes. And like the Board of Directors at Sea World, he had to admit that his father was right about the business upside. "Dad didn't live long enough to see it fully play out for AFTCO," he said, "but his vision and insistence that we give back has greatly benefitted the company."

The best example is AFTCO's business relationship with Guy Harvey, a marine wildlife artist whose renderings, typically of ocean fishes in their natural habitats, have been featured on AFTCO shirts since 1999. AFTCO had been eager to win a license agreement with Harvey, as were other clothing manufacturers with comparable expertise in manufacturing and sales. "We had a good business case to make," Bill said. "But what made AFTCO unique was the passion that our company has for marine conservation, because it was a passion that Guy Harvey shared." The artist, a Ph.D. in marine biology, had started both the Guy Harvey Ocean Foundation and the Guy Harvey Research Institute at Nova Southeastern University.

"The most important thing that ever happened to the growth of AFTCO's clothing business was the opportunity to work with Guy Harvey," Bill said. They collaborated on conservation projects too. Most memorably, Bill was on the boat with Harvey the day that he dove into the water to attach a line to a

1,200-pound black marlin so that a sonic tag could be implanted in the migratory fish. "What made us unique was that AFTCO and Guy Harvey shared a passion, ability, and actual productive history on doing good things for the ocean. If Dad and AFTCO had not developed our unique credible reputation in the marine conservation world I don't know that we would ever have had that opportunity to partner with Guy in his clothing."

Although Milt has been gone since 2002, Bill still feels he is working in cooperation with his father as he implements his designs. By the early 1980s, once AFTCO employed enough full-time workers to justify it, Milt set up a plan whereby the company would calculate 10 percent of each employee's pay and place the sum in an investment fund, regardless of whether the employee made any contribution. "The way Dad saw it, they didn't know how to save or invest," Bill said. "Rather than offer a match, knowing some employees fail to take the free money, he structured things so that they had no choice."

One of AFTCO's hardest workers, a woman who only spoke Spanish, told Milt that while she trusted him, she couldn't believe that the plan would work as he said, enabling a warehouse employee to amass a six-figure nest egg. "Maybe for Bill or one of the English-speaking people in the office," she said, "but not for me." She proposed that he increase her wage by 5 percent. "I'd rather have that each week," she said. "It would cost you half as much, so we both win." Milt would have none of it. "The truth is that it's better for you if we do it my way," he said. "So even though it's going to cost me more than what you propose, that's how we're going to do it." Once again, he was controlling but correct: she retired decades later with far more in her investment account than even Milt had predicted.

During boom years, another AFTCO employee wondered why he had friends who claimed to be earning 20 percent on their investment accounts while AFTCO was generating a lesser return with Milt's conservative approach. "After the market crashed everyone understood the value of the course he'd set," said Bill, who kept to the same philosophy. "We do invest wisely and well, but mainly we just always put the 10 percent in every year and stay conservative." In this way, Milt's benevolent paternalism lives on.

Milt will always be associated in Carol's mind with his strong instinct to be a provider for those around him, but never so much that it harmed their ability to thrive as individuals. This quality shaped his parenting and his planning for death. Well into retirement, he would tell his kids that they shouldn't expect a dime when he died, as he intended to provide for his wife and give the rest to UCLA. In the end, he left some money to his children, but only after months of painstaking work with an estate planner, during which he did his utmost to ensure that he wouldn't inadvertently spoil his children or his grandchildren. He also decided that a large gift to his alma mater while he was still alive would do more than anything to encourage the interdisciplinary work that he wanted done in the marine field. As he put it at the time of the bequest in a speech at the campus, "Here at UCLA, departments of atmospheric sciences, geography, mechanical aerospace, and nuclear engineering, social sciences and admiralty law will all be coordinated and brought to focus on designing and implementing a marine sciences educational program."

His 67-foot fishing vessel would serve as a floating classroom. In one program, local elementary school science teachers were trained to build ocean themes into their lesson plans. The hope was to pique the natural interest that youngsters have in the ocean, creating a new generation of conservation-minded citizens at a time when they were less likely to discover smelt by peeking through the rails of the Santa Monica pier.

As Milt's children retire, his adult grandchildren now confront choices, in their families and their careers, about how their grandfather's life, legacy, and lessons apply to their lives. Milt invested in that brood, enjoying the younger generation as surely as any grandfather but seldom indulging in the aimless pleasure of their company. Instead he regarded time together as a fleeting opportunity to pass along hard won wisdom.

"He felt, I've done a lot, I've learned these valuable lessons, and my goal for the rest of my life is to get that information to these kids," one of his grandsons reflected. "And he was tenacious. He could tell that the grandkids didn't always want to hear whatever lesson he thought we needed. He could've had a nice, fun talk with us, ask how school was going, tell us how great we played, and it would've been more pleasant for him. But he felt a responsibility to have the less pleasant interaction, to impart lessons so well that his grandkids could repeat them word-for-word twenty years later."

A Golden Anniversary Lesson

On the eve of Milt and Peggie's 50th anniversary, the couple felt that the occasion called for a celebration more extravagant than any they had ever indulged. At the dinner table, inside corporate board rooms, on stage at awards banquets, and on fishing trips too numerous to count, Milt avowed that marrying Peggie Rich was the best decision that he had ever made. He felt pride in having done so; pride in the fact that he stayed faithful to her; pride that, unlike so many of their Newport Beach neighbors, they never separated or divorced; and pride in the family that they made. Now the many activities of their grandchildren made it difficult to bring everyone together. So they lavished all necessary resources on the luxury they most valued: the whole family's presence on a vacation. The adults arranged for days off work, the kids told coaches and friends that they would be away, and the couple treated everyone to an Alaskan cruise.

For most grandfathers, the voyage would have been pure leisure, and Milt enjoyed plenty of fine meals and other pleasures. But he wasn't going to traverse a remote coast with all his grandchildren as a captive audience without imparting life lessons. The most memorable began when he summoned all the kids to the ship's game room, led them to a row of slot machines, and bankrolled everyone. Other grandfathers had humored their grandkids at those slots, staking them with a quarter or even a handful. Milt gave out $20 rolls, but explained that they weren't competing to hit a jackpot. The winner would be the first to *lose* their money. A competitive bunch, everyone pulled the levers furiously, racing to squander quarters into the slots, for whoever "went broke" fastest would get all the money the other grandkids had left. Milt loved the spectacle of competitive frenzy and the happy excitement of his grandkids as they engaged in it. But he cared more about the fact that they would learn an unforgettable lesson about how easy it is to lose fast while gambling.

In later years, there would be more family cruises and shared memories. But Milt's deliberate approach to grandfathering also gave him a distinct relationship with each grandchild, shaped by their personalities and Milt's attempts, some more successful than others, to reach each youngster on their own terms. As much as Milt's legacies in business, fishing, and conservation shape how he is remembered, these relationships constitute a significant part of his effect on the world.

A New Grandfather

Milt's oldest grandchild, Anna Maria, arrived in 1972. Daughter of Carol, namesake of Maria Mesa, Milt was present for her birth at a Colorado hospital, and always looked forward to her frequent trips to California. "My parents were only married for a few years, so my grandfather was always like a father to me, a constant presence in my life," she said. "He's always been like a beacon for me, and I still think of him every day."

Anna is a toddler in her earliest memory of Milt: he gets down on all fours, puts her on his back, and crawls around chasing the family dog. She remembers him being lighthearted and exuberant. "One of my scariest memories, which gets at his playful yet hard personality, happened when I was four, behind the scenes at Sea World's shark exhibit," she said. "He put me in the shark cage and pretended like he was going to lower it into the water. I lost it. My mom got upset with him, but he was just laughing. He thought it was the funniest thing. He told my mom that he was trying to harden me up."

On summer visits, Anna would eat lunch with her grandfather at Tale of the Whale restaurant. Afternoons were spent at the Balboa Bay Club, where she would be in the pool with her younger sister. "He'd tell us, 'For the next hour, I'll give you a dollar for every lap you swim past 25 laps.' We'd be so tired, but those laps at the end were the moneymakers, so you'd just keep pushing."

As Anna grew, Milt would tell her about the invention of money and the role of the federal reserve, "stuff I wouldn't have been interested in if he had not talked to me about it." They grew closer when Anna attended Scripps College, an hour's drive from Newport Beach, and stayed with her grandparents on weekends. They would go into the kitchen while Peggie watched TV, sneaking ice cream and talking late into the night. "Long before the financial crisis, he was telling me about the over-leverage of consumers and sovereign wealth. When I look back on conversations we had about gold and credit—I joined the investment club and suggested that we look into gold, and everybody thought I was crazy," she remembers. "But we invested in a company I chose, using a pretend portfolio, and it turned out well. I got a lot of confidence in my ability to succeed in business because of my grandfather."

Her passion was art history. Milt would listen when she shared her course work. But he thought a career in business would open up more opportunities for her. "I was chosen for the JP Morgan training program in New York," she said. "But my heart wasn't in it. That's when he finally realized—he was so sweet and gentle, saying that if art history was really what I wanted to do, that I could do it and I could make a business happen. I ended up working at Christie's auction house. He didn't look at me as someone who would be in a traditional female role, someone who would meet a man, have children, and that was it. He saw my assertiveness and curiosity in himself. And he was constantly trying to push me."

Her grandfather's emotional side is one of the traits she liked best. At movies, he would be the only man crying during emotional scenes. "It was so cute, and he would feel very confident about it, not trying to hide it at all," she said. "But I think that he had a lot of trouble with his emotions as a kid. In the war, he went through things that maybe he didn't ever tell anybody, where to survive he simply couldn't give in to his emotions. That made him less understanding of people who couldn't control theirs."

On Anna's wedding day, Milt walked her down the aisle. She still reflects on a pre-wedding conversation she had with both of her grandparents about why they were determined to keep their vows even through the toughest times in their marriage. "As individuals, you die alone,' they told her. "And do you want, Anna, to be 80 and to look back on your life having stopped and started and stopped and started, or do you want to look back knowing you got through and learned from and moved forward with one person?" In Anna's words, "they persevered not because of the children or the social implications, but because they were always curious about what would happen at the end. Their comment to me was that the end proved much more worthwhile, having gone through it together."

She had observed some of the changes in her grandparents' marriage. "Without sounding harsh, because everyone respected him so much, he could've given my grandmother more time," she said. She remembers standing in the kitchen at Kings Road, her grandmother trying to reach Milt on a ship-to-shore radio.

"She would constantly call without being able to connect, and it would be so frustrating. She'd go to the radio, turn it off, walk away, go back, turn it on, turn it off again. You could very much feel the tension in her, wanting him closer. But toward the end he made it up to her. He really did. Anything she wanted to do, anywhere she wanted to go. Even the theater. And it was so sweet to see him change."

That Way of Teaching

Carol's younger daughter, Shannon, remembers the same summer visits to Kings Road. "Among the older grandkids I was the only female that liked doing guy stuff," she said. "So I had an opportunity to do different things with Papa. I grew up thinking of fishing as trout pulled from streams, so ocean fishing was an experience."

Some people took immediately to Milt's strong personality, as Anna did. Others found it overbearing, as Peggie had when they first met. Shannon loved her grandfather as earnestly as her older sister, but their conversations had none of the same easiness. Growing up in Colorado and living abroad for long stints, she spent less time with Milt than most of her cousins, causing Milt to pack the life lessons that he wanted to impart into less time. She saw his playful side less often. "A lot of growing up was listening to what the Shedd side of my family was saying and listening to what my dad's side was saying," she explained. "Instead of keeping them in silos or feeling like I had to choose, I played devil's advocate and found ways that they could dialogue back and forth. I always tried to be sympathetic to the nice things he was trying to achieve, but he could rub you in the wrong way, and I sometimes found it hard to listen. It was easy for me to just shut him down, not let him in. I would listen. But I would argue and try to think about it in a way that helped me."

As she grew older, she would study teaching and conclude that her grandfather's teaching style hadn't been a good fit for her. She wished that he would have positioned himself less often as "the knower" and more often as a coach, listening to who he was trying to reach and crafting questions that led them to the insights he was trying to communicate. His generation, wasn't ever exposed to that way of teaching, she said. Yet he achieved just that trick when talking about the ocean, giving her a sophisticated understanding of the ecosystem.

"He was a different person when he talked about the ocean," she recalled. "He took me to the fish hatchery in Carlsbad, taught me about consumption, population growth, the need to replenish the system. It wasn't a lecture. You were together on a process of discovery. I'll always remember going behind the scenes at Sea World. He saw everything through our eyes—he would spot things that would resonate with me, take us to places that would interest us. He would even remember what we'd done last time and build on it, but it still felt like he was being a companion rather than an instructor."

The ocean added flashes of unselfconscious enjoyment to their relationship. "He was never more carefree, though there are moments of action on a fishing boat that can be very dangerous," she said. "Some of my favorite moments were just physically doing something with him, when everyone was working in sync. You could feel his powerful presence and enjoyment of those moments. When he stepped onto land he turned into a different person who lost that ability to be carefree."

Their biggest fight was rooted in a time when she was living in Brazil while earning a graduate degree. Her job afforded her the ability to pay her own tuition and rent. For that reason, she had a sum of extra money in the bank, her share of the college fund that Milt and Peggie set aside for all their grandchildren.

"All my life I had known that I have a physique that's almost ideal for being a woman in competitive sports. But emotionally, I always felt crippled, like I never achieved as much as I should have," she said. "So I decided I'd train to bike across Alaska. It felt like this thing I needed to accomplish, to prove to myself that I did have the potential that I had always imagined. It combined a difficult physical journey with a need to figure out logistics and an emotional aspect, training in a foreign country without a bicycle." The twelve days she took to complete the ride were among her life's most rewarding. "It helped me to see that I was who I thought, that I could achieve something without other people," she explained. "The one resource I had was a chunk of money to pay for it."

Later, while visiting California, Shannon was asked what she did with her college money. She told Milt about her excursion. "He was so mad," she said. "He didn't blow up. I never saw him do that. But you could tell it hurt him. I pointed out that I paid my own way through grad school. I asked what he'd say if I told him that I spent his money on grad school and my money biking those 1,000 miles. But he didn't listen. Or he tried, but he couldn't hear me. He'd always talked about the need to defer 'happy fun times.' For him, money was about making your savings grow, or having a physical asset. I think he forgot that there are times to invest in yourself. Then Nonnie stepped in and said that we ought to talk about something else, to enjoy the little time I had for my visit."

Had Milt been less controlling or less intent on imparting life lessons; or if Shannon could've found a way to relate her trip to her grandfather, showing him how she had used the 5ps—proper planning prevents poor performance—and controlled her emotions on the road, perhaps the disagreement between them would have softened. She has fond memories of their light-hearted moments together. "He loved the song 'Don't Cry for Me Argentina,' and when it came on he would roll down the windows, turn the radio up, and just belt it out. Moments like that. They were so different and clear and silly. And it wasn't because I was five or eight or ten that I enjoyed that moment. Anyone would've enjoyed that part of him."

One of the silly moments that she liked best involved Peggie. "She was always a very serious person," she said. "And he was so respectful to her, but very playful too. Driving to Sea World in separate cars, he would be sure to get behind her. Then he would inch up and bump her at stoplights. She would get so angry! It would scratch her car. Or she would be afraid of getting in trouble with the police. She would just be silly mad."

Their marriage meant a lot to Shannon. As she explained it, "You don't see couples like them very often. It didn't feel like what you see in the movies. It was real. It was meaningful to me because it showed me what's possible. How did they do it? I don't know. But their marriage gave me a sense of security and a feeling for who he was deep down. If he'd been flippant or disrespectful to Nonnie, if he hadn't been so in love with her, it would've skewed the way that I saw him. Even though there were things that I didn't like, there was that huge thing that was really different and interesting, that I liked a lot. It was important to me, because I always liked Nonnie so much. Even if I thought my grandfather could sometimes be disrespectful to other people, never her. He loved his family so much, and her especially. That meant a lot."

The Measure of a Man

When Peggie was getting bumped by her husband during a car trip, Will, Carol's oldest son, saw things unfold from his grandfather's perspective. "The guys were all in one car," Will said. "And he just drove right up and bumped her! We thought it was the funniest thing in the world. We could see the girls freaking out inside the car. He was just sitting there chuckling."

Will recalled his grandfather as playful yet constantly alert.

"We used to go to this country club to play golf," he said. "He would always take the same way, driving along the edge of the course so that he could be looking for golf balls. If he saw one he would stop and you would get your ass out and get it. It was funny. He loved to hunt, loved to find things. It didn't really matter what it was. A swordfish on the ocean. A golf ball in the gutter." They bonded over those sorts of games and sports. "I was always getting in trouble as a kid, but we could go have a catch. Or he could give me casting lessons. With sports, I could always impress him by doing a bunch of pushups or chin-ups. And he liked to foster competition. Nothing was more fun than beating him at something, though if you got too good, he wouldn't want to play anymore."

Hating to lose is something they shared.

"I had a lot of emotional issues and I couldn't deal with failure. So that's an area that he'd focus on where I didn't get good marks," Will said. Golfing one time, someone said, 'Milt, you're in no position to lecture him about controlling your emotions,' which was funny. But even if he was just watching you compete, trying to test your mettle, it was an opportunity to impress him."

Will competed against his brother, Charlie, who was a year younger, more than anyone else. "Papa would always try to find an area where Charlie had a strength and I had a weakness, to exploit those in setting up contests," he said.

"What he cared about was how you reacted when the chips were down. The way he saw it, we were growing up in a very privileged environment. We weren't going to be tested by The Great Depression. So he had to find a synthetic way to test us to make sure we were going to be strong. His intentions were to make us more self-reliant, better adjusted kids. It was tough, but probably not half as tough as what his kids went through."

At ten or eleven, Will relished being invited on a two-week fishing trip. His grandfather would put him to work—after catching a swordfish, for example, he would instruct Will in how to scrape out a vein that runs along the dorsal bone so that it wouldn't taint the meat. "And he made me a little harpoon," he said. "I would throw it off the back of the boat at flying fish. Once he pointed out a kelp ball and offered $10 if I could hit it." To clean a fish or hit a kelp ball with a spear or win a foot race—it meant a lot, if he was watching.

"Growing up, everybody wanted to please Papa, and if you did, it was the greatest," he said. "Disappointing him was the worst. Once in Mexico I jumped off the boat with my snorkeling mask on. It came off when I hit the water. By the time I realized what had happened it was already sinking. I looked up to see if anyone had seen what was going on. Of course, he's just looking at me shaking his head. And it wasn't even a question of what I would do. I was going to get that mask whatever it took. So I dove down. I got it too. But I didn't know about the pressure. I didn't know about clearing my ears and stuff like that. I came up with a bloody mouth because one of my braces cut my lip. But it was just like, you had to get that mask."

Will didn't understand his grandfather's "hard-assed side" until he was assigned a school report on World War II. As he recalled it, "We sat down in the living room and started talking about it. I remember asking, 'Did you ever have anybody in your sights?' He looked at me like, seriously? Then he started recounting some of his stories. It was like, holy shit, I can't believe that this guy survived. If you'd gone through that, you might not have a ton of patience for stupid behavior you would encounter. He saw lack of discipline get guys killed." Yet Will also felt that some of what made his grandfather special was unteachable. "Some people just have that–I don't know if it's star quality or what. That very powerful personality. When they step into a room, they're the center of attention, they suck all the oxygen out. They have presence. It wasn't like he tried to steal the spotlight. It was just on him."

Milt's sons and grandsons had the pressure of comparing themselves to their grandfather, something no two responded to exactly the same. "He's the measure of a man, at least in this family," Will explained. "As a kid you pretend to be Michael Jordan or Kobe Bryant while you're shooting baskets. In business or life, that's him. He's what success looks like. He was exceptional at so many things. None of us went into the military, so at least we don't have to worry about keeping up with his combat record. But what he accomplished—that's the bar, what you're being compared to. It's not about other people, that's just my standard. Either you do something on par with that or you fall short. He's been gone ten years, but there's still that pressure to measure up."

He added, "I wouldn't have it any other way."

A Longer-Term Perspective

Charlie, the younger of Carol's sons, remembers how his grandfather would transform a scene. He would be playing on the beach with his siblings. Suddenly, Milt would arrive with a big smile, white teeth set off against his tanned skin, wearing just bathing trunks. And he was playful, yet totally in control:

"He'd have this serene smile. But I was aware of his authority. He didn't need to force it. It was clear when you were doing something you shouldn't that you should stop immediately. If I knew I'd done something wrong, I could expect a stern look or even a scolding. He never blew up at us, though there were times when I could sense something awry, that I needed to backtrack or go to my room and let the situation blow over."

As Charlie grew older, their conversations tended toward their shared interest in finance. "He'd teach me about diversification and being conservative with your savings," he said. "He always returned to instant gratification, how there were people who spend lots of money on a nice car or fancy restaurant meals, but they were only getting a temporary fix. With a longer term perspective, they could get a lot more out of their money."

There can be arrogance in telling others how to live, but Charlie said his grandfather put bounds on the things he emphatically insisted upon: "The way in which he was stubborn was when it was clear to him that there was a vital life lesson he knew to be true, a clear distinction between right and wrong, or a situation where he could reverse what he thought was a moral wrong. He wasn't suffocating; he wasn't trying to impose all his notions on me; there was an appreciation of what I found interesting and an eagerness to hear my ideas."

He remembers when Milt, stricken with cancer, attended one of his high school swim practices. "He was quite sick, and he still made it out in his wheelchair with a big smile," he said. "And he wasn't just there to show support. He was concentrating, watching my strokes, seeing how far I was swimming in what amount of time. He never relaxed. I really admired that." He wonders what their relationship would have been like had Milt lived longer. "He was a very important figure in my life but by no means a controlling one. I can look to him for inspiration, but when I made important decisions about where to go to school, what to study, whether to move abroad," he said, "my decisions weren't in response to Papa."

On the other hand, he added, "when I get an email that says that I can receive a cash dividend or use that money to purchase more shares, I think about that notion that you're trying to delay gratification. He helped me to have the ability to budget and benchmark, because the small, incessant accumulation of savings can lead in the long run to a comfortable life."

What surprises him most is how discussions about Milt have evolved. "He was so successful and loved. And when someone dies, you want to respect and venerate them. Everything seems frozen," he observed. "With time there's a thaw. Now people are at ease talking about his traits, good and bad, in a way that treats him like a human rather than a figure on a pedestal. He's still respected, but with more openness to the whole range of different experiences everyone had."

Providing a Track

Cody, the oldest of Bill's four children, liked being with his grandfather on land more than at sea. He was no good at organizing tackle or tying knots. And he got seasick like his uncle. "It isn't that I never had a good time. I caught a puffer fish once that was all puffed up, and I liked going up with him in that 40-foot tower," he said. "He would joke, or maybe he was serious, that he let his eyebrows grow really long and never trimmed them because it gave him good shade when looking for fish. Instead of a hat all he needed were bushy eyebrows."

Fishing aside, Cody shared most all Milt's interests: games, sports, business, competition, investing, math. At 7 or 8 Milt gave him the talk. "He sat me down in his car for like two hours and explained money, starting from cavemen trading goods to the gold standard and the federal reserve," he recalled. "After that, I was always ahead in the economics classes in school. Instead of buying me baseball cards for my birthday he'd buy me a stock. He talked about the importance of getting some shares in quality companies and just holding them. And I'd follow the share price everyday in the newspaper."

On visits to Kings Road Cody learned to play cards. "He taught me bridge, spades, hearts. We played cribbage and gin rummy," he said. "We wouldn't just play, he would talk strategy during the game and afterward he would go over my hands. That turned into praising me or giving me pointers when I played the hand wrong. But he never let me win, not even one time."

During one card game, Milt explained the concept of financial bubbles. "His world view was that the general person isn't smart, that there were a lot of good people in the world, but a lot of dumb bunnies too. He taught me that when the majority of people are saying something, they're usually wrong. So the thing to do was recognize when a bubble was forming and be very conservative about getting out too early. By the time you know you'd better get out it's too late."

At 15, Cody got another talk, this one about his education: "He told me that for every dollar that I saved, he would give me ten dollars to pay for college. So I worked making ten dollars an hour at a tennis club. I saved $6,000 by the time I was a senior. 'Grandpa, I'm looking good,' I told him. 'That's pretty much what Berkeley will cost me.' That's when he told me that he'd pay for college, and now I had some savings. Learning to accumulate it was a good lesson. But he had taught me to save from the beginning. When I was little, I would show him my piggy bank and brag how I saved the money from my Christmas presents. He would be so proud. He got so excited and involved in what was in my piggy bank."

Milt told all his grandkids that having nice things is good, but it isn't for the young, who haven't earned them. "I remember feeling physically guilty a couple of times after he died, buying something and thinking, 'What would my grandpa say if I bought this?' He really instilled that, because he was paranoid about spoiling us," Cody said. "He would say that he was building a track for us. That he was not just going to hand me things, but he would provide a track to run on, this nice track that is open and free. Not a conveyor belt or a road with a car, but a track, so that if I put forth the effort, I could go straight and fast, but no one would push me along."

The Only Thing a Kid Can Give Back

Each year before Christmas, the vessels of Newport Harbor are decked in festive decorations, packed with revelers, and piloted around in a boat parade of lights. Carie, oldest daughter of Bill, has an early memory of going aboard The Sea World and sitting beside a decorative Santa Claus catching a marlin.

"Papa was very loving, but a little scary when I was very young," she said. "I remember holding his binoculars that night. He went, 'Okay Carie,' gripped his hands over mine so I was holding on really tight, and said, 'whatever you do, do not drop these.' I just sat there in fear. I'm sure, looking back, it was only a little bit of time. I was squeezing them, terrified that I would drop them, and I waited until my dad came by before I stood up to safely hand them off. With that kind of thing you were always like, 'Oh no, I don't want to mess anything up.' He never raised his voice at me ever. I don't remember him scolding anyone. You just didn't want to disappoint him. You respected him and looked up to him, so you wanted to do a good job, make him proud. When you're a kid, you're being given everything. You can't give anything back except that."

The pressure could still be unpleasant. "He had a big personality, and I was the shyest of his grandchildren," she explained. "If you sat next to Papa at a family dinner, you knew you were going to get most of the lessons that night. Looking back, you appreciate it. Being 7, you probably weren't too excited. But you still felt that everything he said was true, the same as if it was being read to you out of the Bible."

He told Carie about saving and investing even when she was very young. "He would tell me, 'If you don't buy that sandwich today, you can buy five tomorrow.' I remember being very little and thinking that was silly, that I wouldn't need five sandwiches tomorrow." Once, he took out his investment portfolio. "He showed me the numbers, what he'd put into it, how it had grown ten times. I remember thinking, Wow that's great... But I'm ten, I'm not really concerned about it!"

Later, Milt's support helped launch her career. "He always told me that if I ever wanted to start a business, he would support me. After he passed, I was able to take the money left from my college fund and partner with a friend in a sushi restaurant. So they gave me financial capital, but also emotional support, because you have to have confidence to be a successful business owner. Or to even want to do it. I don't think I would've turned into an entrepreneur if it wasn't for him."

Work For It

Bill's youngest daughter, Christie, was mischievous and outgoing, just like her grandfather. At age 3 or 4, while feeding the ducks in the Back Bay, her older sister, Carie, got bit. Milt and Christie giggled uncontrollably at the sight. When they saw one another they had a special greeting all their own. "We'd say this Spanish phrase that means bumping heads and then just head butt one another repeatedly. It was just a little game the two of us had, and he loved how aggressive I was about it."

Another game involved Milt's golf bag. Each kid could reach blindly inside a pouch, keeping whatever tees, ball markers, and loose change they could grab. "A lot of his games were lessons," Christie said, "but he also just liked making up games." Every kid got an occasional day alone with their grandparents. Christie spent hers attending musicals at the Orange County Performing Arts Center. They saw lots of standards like *Phantom of the Opera* and *Les Miserables*, but she remembers none so fondly as *Evita*. "It was Papa's favorite," she said. "I'll never forget him standing up in his row singing 'Don't Cry for Me Argentina' as they performed."

Christie was a talented softball player and her grandfather was often in the stands. "We never practiced hitting or catching, but he gave me advice, not so much about the sport itself as having good feelings, staying composed, controlling how your competitors perceive you." The lesson she most associates with Milt concerns the importance of hard work:

"When we were too young to even understand what hard work was he was already instilling it in us," she said. "If we wanted something we had to work for it. He raised his kids that way and my parents raised us that way. If we wanted a Gameboy we would do chores, mow the lawn, sell lemonade. It wasn't, 'Here's your allowance.' It was, 'If you wash my car I'll give you 50 cents.' We learned the value of a dollar and how to save if you wanted something. Almost every family dinner, he would bring up his views, and one of them was, 'I'm not going to raise spoiled, rotten kids. If you want nice, fancy things then you better work your tail off and find a way to get that.' It wasn't going to come from grandma and grandpa or mom and dad. That was ingrained. If you wanted to be lazy or live a certain kind of life, you'd be cut off. If you wanted to get an education, they would supply that, but nothing else."

A Man With a Code

Casey, the youngest of the ten grandchildren, knew his grandfather at his most mellow. "I saw him at family holidays, when he was the stoic, wise grandfather figure, and during sporting events, when he was on the sidelines to support you," he said. "But fishing is the thing that Papa and me did most. Doing the thing he loved, I almost always saw him in a happy, nurturing mode."

Almost every year they would go on a week long trip to Guadalupe Island, off Baja California. Casey got the most time with his grandfather the year his dad, Bill, couldn't make it. "There was a ton of preparation, including learning to tie different knots. I remember him testing me, making sure I was competent," he said. "Once the trip started, it was just fun family time. Staying up late to catch bait, getting up bright and early. When I was a kid I wanted to sleep in. Papa was always the first one up. So I got up early too. People talk about fishing as a serious thing for him, but it was always a fun, recreational experience, even with the rigor you'd expect from Papa. He was always mentoring and giving advice, but in those situations he was more like a kid. There was real joy he derived, whether from being on the ocean or getting to pass down knowledge."

In addition to the fishing, there were trips to tag fish and other marine life, where Casey would learn about conservation. He understood his grandfather to be engaged in important work, an impression that was often reinforced by others. "We used to have these big parking lot sales at AFTCO. And I remember meeting an older guy there," Casey said. "He said that he had gotten into marine biology because of my grandfather. He told me, 'He's my hero.' I remember that striking me as so huge, like, Papa must be a big deal if an adult is telling me he's their hero. I had a lot of experiences like that because I was on fishing boats where he was a hero figure. People would tell me, you know, your grandpa is a legend."

Casey heard the same lessons as the other grandkids: "If you believe in something, just prepare well, work hard, and stick to your guns. Remove the emotional side from decisions and don't be influenced by what others do. You see that in a lot of really successful people, stubborn confidence to go their own way, because if there was an easy decision to make or an easy path to really excel, someone would've beat you to it."

He saw that lesson put into practice on the ocean.

"We were rigging squid," he said, recalling one of his last ocean trips with his grandfather, "fishing for white seabass and halibut, and we saw papa spit something out of his mouth. We look over again, and we see him grab a squid by its head and bite off the butt end like he would a cigar, as a better way to put the hook through its back. I remember it so vividly, because it's something we noticed for the first time even though we'd been fishing with him I don't know how many times. It was one of the subtle little things, there were thousands of them, that he would do, that no one else was doing."

Moral lessons also came across by example.

"I was able to see someone who went down some very difficult paths and found success," Casey observed. "Being so uncompromising in your values is not the easiest thing. It's not easy to be brutally honest with people, totally faithful to your family and the organizations you lead. But in my grandfather's life that all worked to his benefit. You saw the relationships he developed, the friends he made, his ability to provide. Maybe the biggest thing about his lessons is that, right or wrong, he stuck to them. He had a moral code that he was following. It's something that he wouldn't deviate from no matter the pressure. In his case, it helped him to succeed. But even if it hadn't, it's the kind of thing that makes the world go around."

Like many of Milt's grandchildren, Casey has experienced the pressure of living up to his grandfather's expectations. Reading letters that Milt wrote home from World War II actually eased that burden. "It was nice to see that letter to Nonnie, where he talked about how nice it would be to run away together for awhile, to live the bohemian lifestyle and travel," he said. "That's as far away from the Papa that's been portrayed to me as you can get. He had this urge to have happy fun times, to do something a little selfish. When I look at a trip I took abroad—I was born in the West in a lucky situation, where I could afford to go travel, to surf in Indonesia, to see a new culture and explore new places. I wasn't there working, though I worked a few hours a week. It was a selfish trip. So it was nice to see that he had those same urges when he was a young man, because it added a human element to his story and gave me this look at a different side of him, one I've experienced too. A 70-year-old Papa would've said, what a spoiled kid, to go on a trip like that when he should be working. A 24-year-old Papa would've been excited about it."

A Huge Hug and Pound on the Back

Steve's daughter, Danielle, spent occasional afternoons with Milt spotting fish from the end of the Balboa pier. "He'd tell me, 'You have a good eye,' which meant a lot," she said. "Sometimes, he even made it into a game where I would get a quarter for every fish I spotted." She doesn't hesitate when reflecting on the most important lesson he taught her. "We have a lot of responsibilities, to our family, to other people in our lives, and to the world. He caused me to look outside myself at a young age, when you're very egocentric," she remembered. "I'd start to think, how are my actions affecting others? He took it a step further. He wouldn't just say, Danielle, you need to act responsibly, but, 'Danielle, you need to act responsibly, now what are you going to do about it?' He wanted each of us to give back with whatever God-given abilities we had. And we knew that we were responsible for that."

He knew early on that Danielle intended to pursue a career in teaching. "He would say, 'You have empathy and compassion, and that's a good thing.' As long as he saw I was working hard, that I wasn't slacking off, that I was using my abilities, he was happy." If they didn't share the same interest in business, "we did share the same heart for helping others in need," she said, "and on that level we had a lot in common."

Whether he encountered Danielle at one of her high school tennis matches or a family gathering, he was always attentive. "Physical affirmation and saying 'I love you' is something that's important to me," she said. "Papa was very affectionate, always ready to give me a huge hug, pound me on the back, and ask, 'How are you sweetie?'" He was supportive as she got older too. "I'll never forget him sitting with my husband and me right before our wedding," she said. "He shared how important finding the right partner was and how lucky he was to have done so. He hoped we would have the same solid marriage built on communication, mutual goals, and trust."

Years later, she is still struck that her grandfather put so high a value on familial relations and conveying moral values to the next generation, never letting material success define him.

"He understood and taught that possessions wouldn't bring true fulfillment," she said. "He wasn't interested in status either. With my grandma it was never, 'this is Peggie, my trophy.' He said, 'This is Peggie, my equal.'" Danielle now feels newly appreciative of how deliberately he worked to convey those values. "As a parent of 4, I see how his tenacity and perseverance towards parenting stemmed from a heart of love," she reflected. "I don't think this is something you are fully able to comprehend until you are older and have children of your own."

A Grandfather in Grief

Steve wrote a reflection on behalf of his son Brandon, who died at age 20 in 1996.

Brandon shared some of the Shedd traits passed on from Papa. He was smart, clever, athletic, independent-minded and enthusiastic. He heard the lectures we all heard from dad about feelings, emotions, and the traits of hard work and preparedness. He held a respectful honor and healthy fear towards toeing the line in dad's presence, and listening to the values and principles dad was willing to repeat to whomever would listen; or for that matter, at times when we were not so willing to hear the Papa mantra again!

Dad and Brandon shared a common interest in fishing and sports. Dad, when not fishing, would come to Brandon's games. Brandon, on occasion, took swordfishing trips with dad. There was enough of a spark in Brandon's natural ability to shoot a basketball or handle a fishing rod to bring a smile to papa and keep the relationship friendly. But Brandon was naturally shy and sensitive and did not share much with his grandfather. The inner struggles of Brandon, as he grew into early manhood, were far and away too difficult for Brandon to share with dad, nor with anyone for that matter.

Brandon struggled with anxiety. At 13 he had his first known panic attack. At that time, he was diagnosed with an anxiety disorder which haunted him until he ended it by taking his life. His struggle to deal with his disorder was too great for a young man to bear. Dad's reaction was consistent with everything about him. His grief and sadness at losing a loved grandson was deeply sincere, his empathy towards me, Terri and Danielle equally compassionate. As the patriarch of our family, he took the lead as he always did. Never was there blame from dad over Brandon's act. Dad was always loving and supporting, yet with a deep-seated, somewhat fatalistic acceptance that in the harsh reality of life, bad things can happen to good people and families. Dad believed that trying to understand why would only be unproductive.

As any loving father and grandfather would, dad at times struggled with the right words of comfort and consolation. Terri and I remember quite well dad's brutal yet truthful Papa-like reaction to Brandon's suicide: 'What a waste,' he said. Dad never viewed Brandon's act as a blemish on the family name, but rather a simple waste of human potential. Other men have succumbed to heartbreak and depressions after a loss so painful.

To his credit and good fortune, Steve said, "Dad never placed pride in self or family above the power and truth that rested in nature and natural law."

Milt at the End

After being diagnosed with terminal cancer Milt's body gave out. He couldn't walk or even stand, but he still had to catch more fish. He was lifted onto a boat and put in a wheelchair secured to the deck so he could have a final day of ocean fishing. Mere days before his death, he asked to be wheeled to a pond at a local golf course to feel the tug of life at the end of the line one last time. It brought joy to his face even then. His final moments with his brother were as poignant. Irv had been best man in Milt's wedding, and they were especially close in their later years. "They spent many hundreds of days fishing on the ocean together—Irv had the mechanical mind and talent to bring many improvements and fixes to Milt's boat, *The Sea World*, and each had a mutual love and respect for the other's unique abilities," Bill said. "Irv came by to visit Dad a few days before he passed. Dad had his eyes open and could still understand what people were saying to him, but had not spoken for a few days, so Irv did all the talking. As Irv said his final goodbye and got up to leave, Dad put his hand out and said, in a raspy and very low voice, 'Love you, Irv.' What a sweet thing it was to witness such love between two brothers."

At Milt's memorial service, old friends came from far and wide. They received a program with Rudyard Kipling's "If" printed on one side.

> *...If you can dream—and not make dreams your master; If you can think—and not make thoughts your aim; If you can meet with triumph and disaster and treat those two impostors just the same...*

> *...If you can force your heart and nerve and sinew / To serve your turn long after they are gone, and so hold on when there is nothing in you, except the Will which says to them: "Hold on"...*

Bill stood at the podium knowing just what his Dad would say: "Billy, I know you're feeling sentimental, but why waste an opportunity to ask all these nice people if they'd be willing to help support the work Hubbs is doing?" And so he asked. Then everyone celebrated Milt's life by sharing stories about him.

A World War II buddy remembered practicing marksmanship with Milt in the weeks on New Caledonia before they saw combat. They also wanted to teach themselves to gauge, by ear, how far away a gun was being fired. "We had a small target set up that we would shoot at from 50 or 75 yards away, and a little hole dug next to it, so the person checking the target wouldn't get shot," Charlie Ross said. "I would jump out of the hole and tell Milt what he was hitting. Well, after a few times of seeing him fire all his bullets right in the center of the target, I figured, there's no use going down in the hole, and I actually stood right by the target and held it with my hand as those bullets were going zip, zip, zip."

"Then," he chuckled, "it was my time to fire. And Milt, being smart, he stayed in the hole." Milt was an outstanding combat officer, he concluded, and was so respected by his men after every promotion that "if he had stayed in the army he would be a general, and there's only one other guy I ever thought that about."

Another story was relayed from the perspective of Dr. Bill Evans, a former president of Hubbs, who liked to tell about the time he realized that Milt just never quit. They were in Alaska carrying out research on beluga whales. Milt located the whales in a corner of a large bay, but they couldn't use their motor to reach them because it would scare them away. Their guide started rowing, but a quarter of the way there, he said that he was tired, that there was no way that they would make it to the whales before the changing tide caused them to swim on their way. Though in his late-sixties, Milt stood up, forced the guide from his seat, and started rowing for an extended time with all of the intensity that he could muster. Finally, he got to the whales—and was so spent, having done so, that Dr. Evans took a photograph of his face that hangs outside his son's office, a portrait of a man at the limits of exhaustion.

Jeff Ascher declared that one word best described his old friend. "Milt was fearless in everything he did," he said. "Whether he was right or wrong had nothing to do with the case!" Most people are materialistic, he continued, "but when you pass, the only real value you leave is the intangible value that you've imparted to the people that you touch. Not many people leave a legacy like Milt did. He succeeded beyond anyone."

Bill's favorite story about his father captured the depth of his greatest passion. It is the one he shared that day with the assembled:

It was told to me by Timmy Houser, a commercial fishing friend of his. They were anchored out by San Clemente Island. After dinner Timmy went down to go to bed. He left Dad with lights over the side, at least three rods going. Four in the morning, Timmy had to take a leak. He was going to go off the stern. In his bewilderment, he sees a hand coming up over the rail at the back of the boat. It disappears and he thinks, 'My God, Milt's gone over.' He starts to run to the back of the boat, and he sees the hand come up again. Now he's actually woken up, he comes up behind Dad without his knowing, and he just watches. Dad was on his hands and knees on the swim step, holding with one arm to the rail so that he could reach out as far as he could and catch some little bait fish, looking at it, like, 'I caught you, you sucker,' and then staring at it like a four year old at his first frog: 'What are you all about? I want to know about you.' Then he'd reach up and grab onto the rail again. He'd wait for another one to go by, and repeat the whole routine. Nobody had more love, drive, or curiosity to figure out what was going on underneath the ocean than Dad.

A Lasting Image

The California mainland is visible from Catalina Island in clear weather, but that Sunday, as a pleasant weekend of constant fishing and diving ended, visibility wasn't nearly 29 miles.

The sky was overcast. Wind gusted up to 30 knots. The two-masted, 38-foot diesel departed for home despite the rough seas, braving ten to twelve foot swells that came in rapid succession, jostling the vessel and causing minor chaos below deck. Cans, plates and paperbacks were tossed about the cabin. Peggie scrambled to stash all the loose objects someplace secure. Chuckie Gardener, then a young deck hand, rushed up on deck to see if his assistance was required at the wheel.

"Over the years, I saw Milt interacting with the ocean too many times to remember them all," he recalled. "But I'll never forget how he looked at that moment, standing on the open fly bridge, the wind driving spray into his face and hair. He looked like he was in heaven — perfectly in his element, plowing through the waves back to Newport Beach. There was no fear. Just pure exhilaration. It was a small craft, so technically we shouldn't have been out there at all. We should have turned around, gone back to Avalon, waited it out. But not Milt. I'm not saying he did anything unwise. He knew his limits. He knew what that boat could do. He wasn't putting anyone's life in danger. Still, I knew from the look on his face that he was meeting nature, daring nature to give him the worst it could give, and really savoring every minute. 'Milt,' I finally told him, 'it's kind of rough down there for Peggie.' Then he remembered himself, smiled, and pulled back a little bit. He was one of a kind."

A Letter To Future Shedd Family Members From Milt Shedd's Children

The three of us were lucky to have a dad who put a great deal of energy into teaching us principles and life lessons, and a loving mom who could let him know when he was pushing too hard. Our own children learned many of those same life lessons directly from Dad, many of which we have reinforced. But what about our grandkids and beyond, and extended members of the Shedd family? How might they get to know and learn from the patriarch of our family and his extraordinary life? This book was written to serve that purpose, a document for both current and future family members.

As biographer, Conor Friedersdorf dug into the details of dad's life. Common threads of values and purpose found in the lives of America's Greatest Generation wove itself into the life and times of our father, a pattern familiar to other children of the Baby Boomer generation born between 1946 and 1964.

Boomers may discover in this book a dad who shared many of their own father's values and strengths. Most had tough fathers and would understand that arguing with your dad, or even a two-way conversation, was simply not done. Thankfully, much has changed. Parents and children often have more open dialogue on a wide range of issues. What has not changed is importance of the principles lived by Dad and other members of his generation. Much can and should be learned from the people who lived through the Great Depression, WWII, the Cold War and the turn of the 21st Century.

Many of the principles Dad taught are summed up in his most often-quoted piece of literature, the poem "If", which you will find following this letter. Dad often told us what was most important was not so much the outcome but the process of doing one's best. He taught us that if we prepare ahead of time, work hard, and don't quit on ourselves or the task at hand, good things will happen. He encouraged us to not get too full of ourselves if things went our way, or too down if they did not—it did not matter what happens to a person but rather how we react to what happens. He often emphasized the importance of controlling our feelings and emotions, as not doing so would lead to bad decisions and results. He taught that doing things that were hard for us and not running from challenges made us both stronger and the difficult task easier with each attempt. He thought that anything of value was worth working for and that if he gave his kids things too easily he would be hurting rather than helping us.

While both Mom and Dad loved each of us equally and unconditionally, they expected us to develop our character on the tough, not always fair field of life experiences. Family provided a safe haven where Mom and Dad could encourage us and prepare us for a challenge, picking us up if we failed, or bringing us back to reality if we became too full of ourselves. While Dad was a man's man, he made it clear that there would be no disrespect to Mom by any of the kids at any time, that she was his partner in everything, and that she deserved enormous credit for all his success. He taught us the value of family where trust and cooperation could best be learned. He taught us that we should not place too high a value on what others thought about us, that what really mattered was our true feelings about ourselves. He cautioned us to be truthful not only to others, but also to ourselves. And he taught us to protect our integrity as our most important personal asset.

We are fortunate to have had Dad and Mom to impart on us the importance of family and to teach us values that will help us to grow both as a family and as individuals. Our family members have had challenges in the past and will continue to have them in the future, just as all people do. However, if we can practice the principles and values dad worked so hard to teach us, our lives and the lives of people around us in this and future generations of Shedds will be better for it.

Steve, Carol and Bill

Conor Friedersdorf

IF
By Rudyard Kipling

If you can keep your head when all about you
Are losing theirs and blaming it on you;
If you can trust yourself when all men doubt you,
But make allowance for their doubting too:
If you can wait and not be tired by waiting,
Or being lied about, don't deal in lies,
Or being hated, don't give way to hating,
And yet don't look too good, nor talk too wise;

If you can dream—and not make dreams your master;
If you can think—and not make thoughts your aim,
If you can meet with Triumph and Disaster
And treat those two impostors just the same:
If you can bear to hear the truth you've spoken
Twisted by knaves to make a trap for fools,
Or watch the things you gave your life to, broken,
And stoop and build 'em up with worn-out tools;

If you can make one heap of all your winnings
And risk it on one turn of pitch-and-toss,
And lose, and start again at your beginnings
And never breathe a word about your loss:
If you can force your heart and nerve and sinew
To serve your turn long after they are gone,
And so hold on when there is nothing in you
Except the Will which says to them: "Hold on!"

If you can talk with crowds and keep your virtue,
Or walk with Kings—nor lose the common touch,
If neither foes nor loving friends can hurt you,

Meeting Triumph and Disaster

If all men count with you, but none too much:
If you can fill the unforgiving minute
With sixty seconds' worth of distance run,
Yours is the Earth and everything that's in it,
And—which is more—you'll be a Man, my son!

Conor,

Thank you for the job you did on this book. You left no stone un-turned. It made a difference that you read books and researched what life was like growing up in the L.A. area from the 1920's on, fighting in the jungles of the South Pacific during WWII, fishing in California and more. You also read numerous files and articles on the founding and history of SeaWorld and interviewed numerous people about dad. Dad often talked about "looking back into the shadows" of a given situation. What he meant by that was to do more than expected or obvious. That is what you did in taking on the task of writing this book. If dad were still with us, he would respect the job you did on this book. Thank you for ac-curately documenting dad's life in a way that both makes for interesting reading, and also makes clear many of his values and principles for future generations of Shedd parents (and possibly parents from other families) to teach their kids.

~Steve, Carol, and Bill

A staff writer at *The Atlantic* and a contributor to the *Los Angeles Times*, Conor Friedersdorf is also the founding editor of the *Best of Journalism*, a weekly email newsletter that highlights outstanding nonfiction. He is an alumnus of Pomona College, where he received a bachelor's degree in politics, philosophy, and economics, and of New York University, where he earned a master's degree in journalism.